Asylum and Other Plays

By

Mark Pearce

impspired@gmail.com

Cover designed by Steve Cawte

ISBN: 978-1-915819-36-9

To Edmond Rostand and Eugene O'Neill
To Henrik Ibsen and George Bernard Shaw

Who Demonstrated That Theater Can Be Literature

OTHER TITLES BY IMPSPIRED

Fractured Echoes –
by Geraldine Fleming

Shinwell -
by David Milner

Children of the Storm –
by Ann Christine Tabaka

Karma Cola -
by Pranab Ghosh

A Phoenix Still Rising –
by Mary Farrell

Layers of Rust and Life –
by Mihaela Melnic

Addicted to Dog Magazines –
by Laura Stamp

INTRODUCTION

These plays have been produced on the New York stage and across the United States. I've seen them performed in proscenium arch theaters, in basements, and in junior high school auditoriums. Now they exist between the covers of a book. They will sit on bookshelves beside the works of Eugene O'Neill and George Bernard Shaw—at least in my private library.

I've had some wonderful productions around the country with some amazing casts. *Asylum* is based on a quote by Ralph Waldo Emerson. During one of its mountings in New York, the lead actor asked me where he could find the quote. The next day I gave him a collection of Emerson's Essays. In the coming weeks, not only did he read the entire volume, but it began passing around among the rest of the cast and crew. During rehearsal breaks, I would see actors and stagehands sitting around reading the works of Emerson. *Swan Song* takes place in an underground bomb shelter. During one of its New York productions, it was performed in a basement space made over to look like an underground shelter. During rehearsals, the actors asked the producer to lock them in the basement overnight so they could get the feel of living in the environment. From California to Virginia, from Tennessee to Massachusetts, each cast has been a unique set of dynamic, creative individuals I would not have met but for the collaborative nature of theater.

Live theater has also given me the opportunity to explore.

Whenever I've had a play mounted, I've typically taken a meandering road trip to the production, then returned home by a different route. I've stood in the Wright Brothers Bicycle Shop and toured Edison's laboratory. I've visited the graves of Doc Holliday and Edgar Allan Poe and watched the sunset over Walden Pond. I've eaten lobster in Maine and oysters in New Orleans, seen Niagara Falls and the Grand Canyon — and sat in darkened theaters watching characters come to life which had previously existed only in the privacy of my own mind.

In New York they wrote: "*Asylum* is an engrossing psychodrama, thought provoking, original in content. It grabs the audience's attention in the opening act and keeps it riveted throughout."

In Texas they said: "The idea of *Swan Song* is so chilling and so audacious as to stir up the emotions of even the most sophisticated theater-goer. This surge of feeling happens the first few minutes into the drama … and remains long after we've left the theater."

But I always knew that plays are more than just the fleeting experience of a particular production. They also stand as literature. When I was very young, I pulled a volume of Henrik Ibsen off the shelf in my family home. I had seen plays onstage before, but this was an entirely new experience, visualizing a stage production in my mind as I read the script.

Now you hold a volume of plays in your hand. You can experience what I discovered with that first volume of Ibsen. When you've finished, you can cherish it on your bookshelf, donate it to your local library, or toss it in the bin at Goodwill—where another reader might discover it. Stage productions are fleeting. A book may be found among the effects of the garage sale your grandchildren hold after you've gone.

So sit back, turn on your favorite reading lamp, and join me in the unique magic of the theater of the mind.

Because theater is also literature.

CONTENTS

ASYLUM

A Play in Three Acts

ACT ONE

Scene One

Scene is the ornate living room in the home of Dr. Peter Koestler. It is tastefully and expensively furnished. One wall is lined with bookshelves, filled with old classics. Expensive oil paintings adorn the other walls. A heavy bust of Michelangelo's David rests on a carved wooden pedestal. Along one wall, an archway leads to the rest of the home.

Peter Koestler sits in the dark wearing a bathrobe and eating a sandwich. A wood fire has burned itself out, leaving only embers to cast a warm, orange glow to the area immediately around the fireplace. A sudden noise draws Koestler's attention to the window. He sees a man's face peering in. The man has a dark mask over his eyes and a leather cap pulled low over his forehead. His chin is covered with a dark stubble of beard and he wears a leather jacket with the collar turned up. He cannot see Koestler in the dark. Koestler watches as the man uses a tool to pry open the window. It makes a slight, creaking sound. The man freezes, listening carefully to the silence. Reassured, he climbs stealthily through the window, carrying a large, black satchel. He pulls a flashlight from his pocket and casts its beam around the room. Koestler watches as the man begins to load valuables into his bag. The burglar turns his flashlight to a large oil painting over the fireplace. He moves quietly toward it, sets his bag down gently, and reaches for the painting.

KOESTLER: It's a reproduction.

This unexpected statement causes the burglar to shout in fright, jump back toward the wall, and grab his chest.

BURGLAR: Who's there?

KOESTLER: Whom were you expecting?

BURGLAR: I have a gun.

KOESTLER: I'm luckier. I have a sandwich.

The burglar picks up the flashlight, which he dropped when he was startled, and aims it at Koestler.

BURGLAR: What's the idea, hollerin' out and scarin' people like that? You can give a guy a heart attack that way.

KOESTLER: Sorry. I just didn't want you to waste your time on a painting that's worthless. You would do much better to take that candelabra. It's real gold, I think.

BURGLAR (*suspiciously*): Say, what are you doing up, anyway? All normal people are asleep now.

KOESTLER: So I've been told. Would you like a

sandwich? *(The burglar shakes his head.)* A drink? (*The burglar does not answer. Koestler moves to the bar, which is in the corner at upstage right. The burglar keeps the flashlight aimed at him.*) You like scotch? (*No answer. Koestler starts fixing drinks.)* There's a light switch over on that wall.

The burglar turns on the light and puts his flashlight away. Koestler hands him a drink.

BURGLAR: Who are you?

KOESTLER: I'm Peter Koestler. Who are you?

BURGLAR: I'd rather not say. (*Looks around.*) You live here?

KOESTLER: Yes.

BURGLAR: And you tell me I should take the candelabra instead of the painting?

KOESTLER: Yes.

BURGLAR: I'll take the painting. (*Moves toward it.*) You better not try to stop me, either.

KOESTLER (*laughing*): I wouldn't dream of it.

The burglar pulls the painting down. Koestler makes no move to stop him.

BURGLAR (*incredulous*): You really don't care if I rob you.

KOESTLER: No. I figure you must need what you take worse than I do.

BURGLAR: How do you figure?

KOESTLER: Because I wouldn't steal it.

BURGLAR (*sets painting down*): You're strange.

KOESTLER: So I've been told.

Koestler sits on the couch and watches as the burglar begins to load valuables into his bag once again. As he does this, the burglar begins to awkwardly make conversation.

BURGLAR: Nice place you got.

KOESTLER: Thank you.

BURGLAR: You live alone?

KOESTLER: My sister and her son live with me. They moved in after her husband died.

BURGLAR: Oh. (*There is an awkward silence, then the burglar scowls at Koestler.*) This is ridiculous! Why can't you be robbed like a normal person?

KOESTLER (*standing*): What would you have me do? Shout? Faint? (*He suddenly grabs up the bust of David.*) Stave in your skull?

BURGLAR (*quickly*): No, no, no. Nothing like that. (*Koestler grins and sets the bust down.*) I'm just saying you shouldn't be offering me drinks and treating me like I was a guest.

Koestler sits. The burglar starts to grab some things off a shelf, then, as an afterthought, he moves the bust out of Koestler's reach.

KOESTLER: Just because you're robbing me is no reason we can't be friends. Have a seat. Let's talk awhile. You must be tired from a night's work, and I would be fascinated to hear what it's like to be a burglar. (*The burglar sits uncomfortably.*) So tell me, what made you decide to be a felon.

BURGLAR: I dunno. Beats working. . . I guess I like the hours. . . I dunno. . . What do you do?

KOESTLER: I'm retired.

BURGLAR: That must be great. You do a lot fishing?

KOESTLER: Not really.

BURGLAR: That's what I'd do if I had the time. I especially like to fish at night. You can just sit back and watch the stars.

KOESTLER: You like to watch the stars?

BURGLAR: Sure.

Koestler goes to the window.

KOESTLER: Come here. I want to show you something. Look out there, between those two buildings. See the three stars in a triangle? (*The burglar nods.*) See that bright star above them?

BURGLAR: Yeah.

KOESTLER: That's *my* star.

BURGLAR: *Your* star?

KOESTLER: Yes. That bright one right there.

BURGLAR: How did it get to be *your* star?

KOESTLER: I don't know. One night it just seemed to be calling out to me. Singing. That's the night I went mad.

BURGLAR: What?

KOESTLER: I said that's the night I went mad. I'm insane, you see. (*The burglar edges toward the door. Koestler grips his arm.*) Don't leave. I'm harmless. My psychiatrist practically guarantees it.

BURGLAR (*trying to twist free*): Look, mister, I need to be heading home. It's getting early. You can keep your painting and your candelabra and everything else, but I need to be going. (*He pulls free and starts out the door. Stops suddenly.*) Hey, there's a cop coming this way.

KOESTLER (*looking out*): That's Officer Jameson. (*Starts to wave.*) Hello—

The burglar pulls him back.

BURGLAR: Hold on. We don't want to attract his attention.

KOESTLER: I think you would like him.

BURGLAR: I doubt it. Look, why don't we just stay in here and talk some more?

KOESTLER: Okay.

They move to sit down. Just then, Officer Jameson knocks and opens the door.

COP (*entering*): Good morning, Peter. I noticed your light. . . Oh, I didn't know you had company.

KOESTLER: Just a friend. Let me introduce you. This is Officer Jameson. Jameson, this is . . . uh . . .

BURGLAR (*abruptly*): Mr. Smith.

COP: Pleased to meet you. (*The burglar reluctantly takes the hand that is offered.*) I'm always glad to meet any friend of Peter's. Are you a business acquaintance?

KOESTLER: Mr. Smith is an art collector.

COP: That sounds interesting.

BURGLAR: It is.

KOESTLER: Can I get you something to drink?

COP: No, thank you. I'm still on duty.

BURGLAR (*extremely nervous*): I could use another.

KOESTLER (*smiles*): Of course. Help yourself. (*The burglar goes behind the bar.*) How's Martha's cough?

COP: Much better. The medicine she's taking has helped a lot.

KOESTLER: Good.

BURGLAR (*coming from behind bar*): You're out of ice.

KOESTLER: There may be some in the kitchen. It's right through there.

Burglar exits quickly, stage right.

COP: He seems like a nice guy.

KOESTLER: He is.

COP: One thing I'm curious about, though . . .

KOESTLER: Yes?

COP: Um . . . Have you ever noticed that, um . . . Mr. Smith wears a mask?

KOESTLER (*smiles*): He like to remain incognito.

COP (*smiling*): I guess I never will get used to your friends. Remember the boy who thought he could fly?

KOESTLER: Yes. He got out of the hospital just last week.

COP: Good. You know, when he was up on that roof, just as he jumped off, there was this intense look of determination, and for a moment, just a moment, I thought he might make it.

KOESTLER (*laughing*): I remember. You yelled, "Come on, boy, flap!"

They both laugh.

COP: He's lucky he only broke a leg.

KOESTLER: He said that from now on he's only going to take off from the ground.

COP (*laughing*): Good. (*Pause, then seriously.*) Say, how's your nephew?

KOESTLER: The same as always.

COP (*seriously*): Oh.

KOESTLER (*smiles, puts his hand on Jameson's shoulder*): Still worried about me?

COP: I can't help it. He's no good, that one. You better watch him.

KOESTLER: I'm not worried.

COP: Just be careful.

KOESTLER: I will.

The burglar enters with the ice. He is in a state of great agitation.

BURGLAR: Did you know your back door is jammed and the windows are painted shut?

KOESTLER (*smiles*): Yes.

BURGLAR: What if someone had to get out in a hurry?

KOESTLER: I guess he'd be trapped.

COP: Why would you be checking the door and windows?

KOESTLER: Mr. Smith is a security expert. I do need to fix that door, though. My sister was going to call someone, but I think we can do it ourselves.

BURGLAR: That reminds me, is your sister an especially nervous woman?

KOESTLER: Sometimes. Why?

BURGLAR: Because there is an especially nervous woman in the kitchen.

KOESTLER: Uh, oh. I'd better see to her.

Koestler exits quickly, stage right. The burglar and the cop are silent a moment. Then—

COP: You look familiar.

BURGLAR: I'm not.

COP: You remind me of someone.

BURGLAR: I'm trying not to.

COP: Could I have seen your picture someplace?

BURGLAR: No chance. I have my picture taken as seldom as possible.

COP: I'm almost certain . . .

BURGLAR: Look, it must have been some other guy.

COP: I guess. You're not nervous, are you?

BURGLAR *(too quickly):* No. Why?

COP: I don't know. You just seem a little on edge. (*Pause. He smiles.*) I know. He told you he's crazy, didn't he?

BURGLAR: Yes.

COP: That's just what the psychiatrists think.

BURGLAR: They should know.

COP: Don't you believe it. Just because he hears the stars sing and talks to animals . . .

BURGLAR: I guess that's not so strange. Lots of people talk to animals.

COP: Koestler asks their advice.

BURGLAR: Oh.

COP: I think it's refreshing.

BURGLAR: I think it's strange.

COP: How long have you known Dr. Koestler?

BURGLAR: *Doctor* Koestler?

COP: Sure. He's a PhD. Regular genius. At least he was before he lost his mind.

BURGLAR: I didn't know that. We just met.

COP: You'll get used to his eccentricities after a while. He saved my job once. Have him tell you the story sometime. I have to be getting back on my beat. You'll say goodbye for me, won't you?

BURGLAR: Sure.

COP: Thanks. I'll see you around.

BURGLAR: Yeah. Goodbye.

Exit Jameson. The burglar sips his drink and watches the archway at stage right. Enter Koestler.

KOESTLER: Jameson gone?

BURGLAR: Yeah. Now listen here, buddy. I'm through fooling around. Lunatic or no lunatic, I came here to do a job, and I'm going to do it.

KOESTLER: Fine. (*The burglar begins loading things into his bag once again.*) Need any help?

BURGLAR (*agitated*): No, I don't need any help.

KOESTLER: I just thought you might be interested to know that there's a wall safe behind that picture.

The burglar jumps to it, removes the picture, and goes to work. He pulls out a nail file and rubs his fingertips to make them more sensitive. Then he begins to work the dial. From time to time he tries the handle to see if the safe will open. As he works, he begins to talk to Koestler.

BURGLAR: Listen, I'm sorry I scared your sister.

KOESTLER: That's okay. She's beginning to get used to me and my friends.

BURGLAR: Is she the one who supports you?

KOESTLER (*smiles*): Not exactly.

BURGLAR: Then who paid for this place?

KOESTLER: I did.

BURGLAR: You must have made a lot of money before you went . . . uh . . . before you . . . um . . .

KOESTLER: Lost my mind?

BURGLAR: Yeah.

KOESTLER: I earned a living.

BURGLAR: If you paid for this place, you did more than just earn a living.

KOESTLER: I've always excelled at whatever I've tried. Even insanity.

The burglar tries the handle of the safe. It won't open.

BURGLAR: Look, I haven't got all night. What's the combination?

KOESTLER: 16 right, 42 left, 72 right, and open.

The burglar opens the safe.

BURGLAR: Hey, there's nothing in here!

KOESTLER: I know.

BURGLAR: You told me—

KOESTLER: I told you we had a wall safe behind the picture. I didn't say we keep anything in it.

The burglar sits down and starts to laugh.

BURGLAR: I give up. You win.

KOESTLER: How do you mean?

BURGLAR: I mean you got through to me. I like you, Koestler.

KOESTLER: Thanks.

BURGLAR: Were you like this before?

KOESTLER: No.

BURGLAR: The cop told me you were a real genius. What happened? Your brain overload?

KOESTLER: Something like that.

BURGLAR: Were you a scientist before?

KOESTLER: I've been a lot of things in my time. Scientist. Businessman. . . . Lunatic. . . . Now I'm an angel. That's the form of my insanity. I see through the mist which hides the Paradise around us.

BURGLAR: An angel?

KOESTLER: Yes. Emerson once said that the world is an asylum for angels with amnesia. He said that every once in a while, one of these angels will begin to regain its memory and from this comes our great art and literature and music. These are fleeting glimpses of what it's like in Heaven. If so, then the angel called Emerson was almost well. . . . And the angel called Peter Koestler has finally gone sane.

BURGLAR: So what do you do now?

KOESTLER (*somberly, as though to himself*): I sit in the middle of an asylum of insane angels and wait for my release.

BURGLAR: It must be hard.

KOESTLER (*still as though to himself*): Not really. (*Recovers himself, speaks brightly.*) I see myself as a sort of trustee. In my own small way, I help guide others to their sanity.

The burglar starts to laugh, then an idea occurs to him which turns him serious.

BURGLAR (*earnestly*): Don't ever let them cure you. The psychiatrists, I mean.

KOESTLER: Cure me? Why would they want to do that?

BURGLAR: It's their job.

KOESTLER: Their job is to keep me crazy enough to need their services but sane enough to keep from killing them. No, it looks like I'm a lunatic for the duration.

BURGLAR: I'll drink to that. (*They go to the bar.*) I worked in a bar once.

KOESTLER: Really?

BURGLAR: Yeah. Over on Eighteenth Street. Place called Ted's. I don't work there anymore, though. Now I'm my own boss. (*He hands a drink to Koestler.*) Hey, you know any songs?

KOESTLER: Plenty.

BURGLAR: Like what?

KOESTLER: Just start one. If I don't know it, I'll fake it.

The burglar starts to sing. Koestler joins in. They get louder and more lively as they go. The burglar even begins to improvise a little jig. When they are at their peak, Jack Dailey enters, stage right. He is the tall, slender nephew of Koestler. He is appalled at the spectacle of his uncle and the burglar.

DAILEY: What is going on here?

BURGLAR: We're having a party. Let me fix you a drink, pal.

DAILEY (*coldly*): If I want a drink, I'll fix it myself. (*to Koestler*) Mother is having a fit.

BURGLAR (*sensing the sudden change in climate*): Maybe I

better go.

KOESTLER: You can stay. Jack doesn't mean it.

DAILEY (*to burglar*): My uncle is not responsible for his actions. He has no right to invite you in here. Are you going to leave, or am I going to have to call the police?

BURGLAR: Come to think of it, I do have business elsewhere this morning.

He begins to gather his things.

KOESTLER: You sure?

BURGLAR: Yes. I'm really late. I was just going to leave anyway.

He starts to pick up the painting. Dailey looks at him sharply. He sets it down, heads for the door, then turns to Koestler.

BURGLAR: If you ever want to look me up, come down to Ted's on Eighteen Street and ask for Jim. Everybody knows me.

He exits.

DAILEY (*contemptuously*): Eighteenth Street. I might have known.

KOESTLER: You shouldn't have sent him away.

DAILEY: He had no business being here.

KOESTLER: He's my friend.

DAILEY: He was just taking advantage of your good nature, Uncle Peter. He left quickly enough when I mentioned the police.

KOESTLER (*his voice dangerous for the first time in the play*): If you're not careful, Jack, I just might be forced to regain my sanity.

DAILEY: You know that nothing would make me happier.

They stare at each other, then Dailey looks away.

KOESTLER: I'm going to get dressed. If I hurry I might be able to catch up with Jim.

DAILEY: Just don't bring him back here.

Koestler exits, stage right, without answering. Dailey goes to the bar and begins to fix himself a drink. Ann Dailey peeps in, stage right.

ANN: Is that man gone?

DAILEY: Like leaves before a hurricane.

ANN: You shouldn't drink so early in the morning.

DAILEY: It doesn't bother you that my uncle drinks this early, Mother.

ANN: Your uncle has special problems. It's not easy being insane.

DAILEY: I hope that now at least you realize something has to be done.

ANN: I know you're right. I just don't know if he'll go for it.

DAILEY: You know he'll do anything you ask him to. And you had better hurry. The longer he remains legally responsible for himself, the more chance there is of him getting into trouble.

ANN: I know.

DAILEY: And that's not all. Did you know that he's beginning to give money away in large quantities?

ANN: I think he mentioned something.

DAILEY: And you didn't tell me? How do you expect me to keep us solvent with him giving money away all the time?

ANN: It is his money. He worked hard for it. Dr. Bates even thinks that his condition may have been brought on by overwork.

DAILEY (*contemptuously*): Overwork. All he ever did was luck into a couple of discoveries which proved financially lucrative. The hard part of the business is the running of it, which is what I have to do because he is too lazy—pardon me, crazy—to do the work himself.

ANN: That's not fair, Jack. Peter is a great man.

DAILEY: Was. Now he's sick.

ANN: He won't always be like this.

DAILEY: Exactly. Someday he's going to be well. Until then, we can't let him squander his fortune. You've got to get Uncle Peter to sign custody of himself over to you. Then he won't be able to cash any checks without your endorsement.

ANN: Isn't there some other way?

DAILEY: No. Phil said that since Uncle Peter is not dangerous, the only way we can get custody of him is for him to sign it over. I've already had Phil draw up the papers.

ANN: I won't have Peter locked up.

DAILEY: You won't have to. In fact, this will prevent that sort of thing. This will make you legally responsible for his actions.

ANN: And you have the papers here?

DAILEY: They're on my desk. This is the only way, Mother. This morning's incident should prove that. Inviting a hoodlum into our home and treating him like an honored guest. There's no telling what Uncle Peter might do.

ANN: All right. I'll talk to him.

DAILEY: Good. I'm going to go upstairs. It will be better if I'm not around. Don't worry. When he regains his sanity, he's going to be grateful.

Exit Dailey. Ann paces and wrings her hands. Enter Koestler. He is fully dressed now.

KOESTLER (*cheerfully*): Hi. Feeling better?

ANN: Yes, much.

KOESTLER: That's good. You shouldn't worry about my friends. They may be unusual, but they're nice. (*Kisses her on the cheek.*) I'm going out for a while. You want me to pick you up anything?

ANN: No. But I would like you to do something for me before you go.

KOESTLER: Anything.

ANN: I'd like you to sign this.

KOESTLER (*takes it and glances through it*): What is it?

ANN: It's just a legal document. It makes me legally responsible for you.

KOESTLER: What? (*Suddenly on guard.*) Was this Jack's idea?

ANN (*earnestly*): I don't know why you dislike him so. He's so concerned about you, and you seem to hate him.

KOESTLER: I don't hate him, Ann. It's just that he sometimes tries to take advantage of people.

ANN: Do you think I'm trying to take advantage of you?

KOESTLER: No, Ann. Not at all.

ANN: Then please sign this. If you do something wrong now, you will be sent to prison because you are still legally responsible for your actions. I couldn't take that.

KOESTLER: You don't have to worry about me. I won't do anything wrong.

ANN: Please sign it, Peter. It would be such a relief to me. It's no good like this, Peter. Please?

KOESTLER: This is just another one of Jack's schemes.

You know he wants to have me put away.

ANN: These aren't commitment papers.

KOESTLER: No, but this is the first step. Once I sign custody over to you, I'm helpless.

ANN: Peter, you're ill. You do strange things.

KOESTLER: Does that mean I need to be locked up?

ANN: I'm not talking about locking you up.

KOESTLER: It wouldn't be long before Jack would be pressing a set of commitment papers on you and telling you that I need to be protected from myself.

ANN: I would never have you put into an asylum. You know that, don't you?

KOESTLER (*gently*): Yes.

ANN: Then please sign this.

KOESTLER: Is it that important to you?

ANN: Yes.

KOESTLER: Okay.

He signs. She kisses him on the cheek.

ANN: Now it will be like when we were small and I used to take care of you. Remember?

KOESTLER: I remember. (*Kisses her.*) I have to be leaving now. I'll be back later.

ANN: Will you be in time for lunch?

KOESTLER: Probably. If I'm not back, start without me.

ANN: Okay. Goodbye.

KOESTLER: Goodbye.

Exit Koestler. Ann sits smiling after him. Then she picks up the legal document he has just signed. Enter Dailey.

DAILEY: Did he sign?

ANN: Yes.

DAILEY: Good. (*He takes the document.*) Wait a minute!

ANN: What's wrong?

Dailey rushes to the door and calls out.

DAILEY: Uncle Peter! Uncle Peter!

ANN: Jack. What's wrong?

Dailey turns back to her.

DAILEY: Here's what's wrong. (*He hands her the paper. She begins to laugh.*) Imagine the gall.

ANN (*laughing*): At least he spelled your name right.

Curtain

ACT ONE

Scene Two

Same scene as before, several days later. Ann sits reading. There is a knock at the door. She rises to answer it. Enter Phil Burroughs.

ANN (*delighted*): Phil! Hello.

She hugs him.

PHIL: Hello, Ann. How have you been?

ANN: Fine. And you?

PHIL: I'm doing all right.

ANN: Come on in and sit down. Peter isn't here right now. He's out with a friend of his.

PHIL: I came to see Jack.

ANN: I'm afraid he's at work. He should be home for lunch soon, though.

PHIL: I don't mind waiting.

ANN: Would you like some coffee?

PHIL: No, thank you. I'm fine.

ANN: This is such a surprise. You almost never visit us anymore.

PHIL (*uncomfortable*): Well, I've been overworked lately. A lot of cases have been coming in, and we're breaking in a new clerk. And you know the—

ANN: Phil.

PHIL: What?

ANN: You don't have to explain.

(*Pause*)

PHIL: How is he, Ann?

ANN (*hesitantly*): He's all right.

PHIL: Is there any chance that he might be getting better?

ANN (*lowers her head*): No. (*Pause, then quietly.*) Sometimes I wish he had stayed at the university.

PHIL: He couldn't. Peter was always too ambitious.

ANN: He's not ambitious now. (*Looks up at Phil.*) He misses you. You're his best friend, you know.

PHIL: I know.

ANN: I think it hurt him, what you tried to do with those custody papers.

PHIL: Has he said anything?

ANN: He said you had planned to use them to have him put away.

PHIL: Is he angry?

ANN: No. (*smiles*) Jack was mad, though. Did you know Peter signed his name?

PHIL (laughs): Yes. I started to have Jack committed just so it wouldn't be a total loss.

Ann laughs. Koestler appears at the window. He uses a burglar's tool to trip the latch. Ann and Phil watch him as he crawls through the window.

KOESTLER (*excited*): Phil! I didn't know you were coming by today.

PHIL: Hello, Peter.

KOESTLER: What's wrong? Oh, the window. I was just trying out something my new friend taught me. He's a very talented individual.

PHIL: Undoubtedly.

KOESTLER: Ann, have you asked Phil to stay for lunch?

ANN: No. (*Turns to Phil.*) But you're certainly welcome.

PHIL: I'd like to, but I have another commitment.

Peter: You can stay awhile, though, can't you?

PHIL: For a while.

ANN (*rises*): I know you two have a lot of catching up to do, so I'll just leave you alone. It was nice talking to you, Phil. I hope you'll visit more often.

PHIL: I'll try. (*Exit Ann.*) Your sister is a charming woman.

KOESTLER: I know. She's a true angel.

Phil is made uncomfortable by the word "angel," but he tries to hide it.

PHIL: How have you been, Peter?

KOESTLER (*smiles*): As well as might be expected for someone who's deranged.

PHIL: Stop it!

KOESTLER: What?

PHIL: You know what I'm talking about.

KOESTLER (*quietly*): That's true.

PHIL: Then why?

KOESTLER: Why does it bother you so much, my being an angel.

PHIL: Because it's not true. Just look in the mirror. You'll see a very good man, but no angel. And look out the window. That's no paradise out there.

KOESTLER: Maybe you're not looking hard enough.

PHIL: Peter, I've been your best friend for as long as I can remember. Let me help you. (*desperately*) There must be some way I can reach you. I know you're still inside there somewhere.

KOESTLER: You're really bothered by my condition, aren't you? (*Phil nods.*) Come with me today when I go to the park. I'd like you to meet some of my friends. Maybe you can begin to understand.

PHIL: I can't today. I have to work.

KOESTLER: You can miss one day.

PHIL: This may not mean anything to you, but I have responsibilities. There are people who count on me doing my job. If I waste a day, they're the ones who suffer.

KOESTLER: Perhaps this weekend.

PHIL (*vehemently*): Peter, you've got to stop frittering your life away. Don't you see what you're doing?

KOESTLER: Clearly.

PHIL: Jack tells me you've been giving money away.

KOESTLER: Only to people who need it desperately.

PHIL: What about your own family? They have to live, too. Jack said you're giving away more money than your investments are bringing in.

KOESTLER: Jack seems to forget that the money I give away is my own.

PHIL: And what are you going to do when the money runs out?

KOESTLER: It won't. Let's change the subject. You say you can't take the afternoon off, then at least cancel your luncheon engagement so you can have lunch here. I can make some sandwiches and we can—

PHIL: No, thank you. I'm not planning on eating lunch today. My engagement is a business meeting. I have to—

He is cut short when Dailey enters.

DAILEY: Hello, Phil.

PHIL: Jack.

KOESTLER: How was your morning, Jack?

DAILEY: Just fine.

PHIL: Say, Peter. I think I will have that sandwich after all.

KOESTLER (*brightly*): Good. You want one, Jack?

DAILEY: No, thank you.

KOESTLER: Okay. I'll be back in just a minute.

He exits.

DAILEY: Well, what did you find out?

PHIL: Peter owns fifty-three percent of the stock. There's no way you can take over.

DAILEY: Come on, Phil. I run that company. There must be some way for me to get control.

PHIL: Unless he's willing to sell some of his stock . . .

DAILEY: I'm not talking about buying.

PHIL (*ironically*): I know.

DAILEY (*vehemently*): The man is ruining the business. All the money we make is being thrown away; given to hospitals, summer camps, diseases. Anybody with their hand out winds up here. Can't you do something?

PHIL (*slowly*): Maybe I can.

DAILEY (*excited*): You've got something?

PHIL: Maybe. We both want something here. You want control of your uncle's company. I want him to get the help he needs.

DAILEY: So what do we do?

PHIL: If you give me authorization to have Peter's case reviewed, I may be able to have him committed to a hospital for treatment.

DAILEY: You can do that?

PHIL: Yes, if I can get two psychiatrists to agree he needs medical help.

DAILEY: What are the chances of that?

PHIL: Dr. Bates has already agreed. He's going to talk to

a Dr. Reid who runs a sanitarium in Fairfield. That's only twenty miles from here, so if we have him committed there, you and Ann will be able to visit him often. Bates is going to show Reid the video tapes of his sessions with Peter.

DAILEY: And if Uncle Peter is committed, then I'll have control of his company?

PHIL (*disgusted*): Shut up, Jack.

DAILEY: What's wrong with you?

Koestler enters, carrying a plate with several sandwiches on it.

KOESTLER: Here we are. I made one for you, Jack, just in case you change your mind.

He sets the plate down and starts handing out the sandwiches. The lights quickly fade.

ACT ONE

Scene Three

Scene is Dr. Reid's office. Furnishings are simple and dignified: desk, chairs, couch, bookcase. As scene opens, Nigel is sitting on the couch, his legs pulled up to his chest. He is 20 years old, slender, timid. Dr. Reid sits in a chair.

REID: You've been showing some nice improvement, Nigel. You're calmer than you used to be, and you're more stable. However, you're still resisting treatment. Your refusal to communicate is detrimental to your development. (*Pause*) This will be so much easier if you will cooperate. You know you will eventually. (*Pause*) Very well. (*He goes to the door, opens it, and speaks to someone in the outer office.*) Ms. Opel, would you send Harry in here? (*He pulls a notebook out of his shirt pocket, writes in it, and addresses Nigel.*) I'm scheduling you for three treatments next week. (*Pause*) Don't be discouraged, Nigel. You are getting better. We just have to keep at it.

Enter Harry.

HARRY: You wanted me?

REID: Yes. Take Mr. Tonn back to his room.

HARRY: Yes, sir.

Harry escorts Nigel out. Reid goes to his desk and starts to do some paperwork. Enter Nurse Sharon Opel carrying a pad, a folder, and a large book.

OPEL: Here's the file you wanted to see on Lester Moss, and I found that case history on Theodore Jennings. I marked the place.

REID: Thank you. (*He opens the book and starts to glance over the article.)* Were there any calls during the session?

OPEL: Yes. (*Consults her pad.*) Mrs. Limer called twice in reference to her son. She wants to visit him next week. I told her I would check back with her.

REID: I suppose it could be arranged. (*Checks desk calendar.*) Tell her she can come on Tuesday.

OPEL (*making note*): Yes, sir.

REID: Any other calls?

OPEL: Mr. Switzer from the government office called.

REID: Is it that time again?

OPEL: I'm afraid so. He'll be here next Thursday to inspect the hospital and review our treatments.

REID: I don't see how they expect us to be innovative if we're always having to justify our procedures to a man with absolutely no background in psychiatry. Okay, who else?

OPEL: A Mr. Anthony called. He wants to talk to you about having his mother committed here.

REID: I hope you explained we're over capacity now.

OPEL: I did, but he was quite insistent. I told him I'd have you call him.

REID: Okay. Anyone else?

OPEL: No.

REID: Good. I don't know how much longer we can continue with this workload. You'd think we were the only hospital in the state. I think I'm going to start training Harry to give the patients their preliminary tests. Maybe that will take some of the load off Dr. Knowles and myself.

OPEL: Do you think Harry can handle it?

REID: Sure. There's nothing to it. All he has to do is administer the tests and record the results. Maybe I could add another doctor to the staff. The trouble is, it's so hard to find anyone with enough intelligence and ambition. I feel as if I'm working in a vacuum.

The phone rings. Opel answers.

OPEL: Dr. Reid's office . . . One moment, please. (*to Reid*) It's Dr. Bates. He wants to know if you've finished with the tapes of his sessions with Mr. Koestler.

REID: Not yet. See if you can schedule a meeting for next Friday. I want to discuss some things with him personally.

OPEL (*into the phone*): Dr. Bates? Dr. Reid was wondering if you might have some time available on Friday . . . Two-thirty? That would be fine . . . Thank you. Goodbye.

She hangs up, then turns to Reid.

REID: Does he want me to go there, or will he be coming here?

OPEL: He'll be coming here.

REID: Good.

OPEL: Will I be attending the meeting?

REID: Yes. I want you to view some of the tapes before then. I think you'll find Mr. Koestler is a remarkable case. He was a brilliant man before his illness. Now he says he's an angel, and claims the world is a paradise. (*angrily*) That Bates is doing him no good at all. He lets Koestler run him around in circles. Koestler is sharp. Make no mistake about that. Bates is only compounding the trouble.

OPEL: You seem genuinely upset.

REID: I am. Men like Bates do a great deal of damage. Koestler needs help, and instead he just winds up paying medical fees. (*Pause*) I can't imagine anything more horrible than a great mind gone mad. When I think of the tremendous waste . . . To consider what Koestler has been. And what he might yet become . . .

OPEL (*smiles slightly, with gentleness and affection*): You're going to have him committed here, aren't you?

Pause, then Reid slowly turns to her.

REID: Absolutely.

Curtain

ACT ONE

Scene Four

Peter Koestler's living room, two weeks later. Dailey enters, carrying a newspaper. He seems excited, worried. He sets the newspaper on his desk and goes to the archway at stage right.

DAILEY: Mother! Could you come out here a minute?

He starts pacing. Ann enters.

ANN: What's wrong, Jack?

DAILEY (*stops pacing*): Nothing's wrong. Is Uncle Peter upstairs?

ANN: He went out to mail a letter.

DAILEY (*agitated*): Why did you let him go? I told you I wanted him here when I got home.

ANN: He won't be gone long. (*Dailey goes to the window and looks out.*) Jack, something is wrong. Is Peter in any trouble?

DAILEY (*abrupt, harsh*): No. He's not in any trouble.

ANN: Why are you so edgy?

Dailey hesitates, then his resolve grows firm.

DAILEY: Mother, we have to talk.

ANN (*frightened*): He is in trouble.

DAILEY: Don't get excited. Uncle Peter is okay.

ANN: Then what?

(*Pause*)

DAILEY: Phil is having Uncle Peter committed to a mental hospital.

ANN: No!

DAILEY: Don't get excited, Mother. If Uncle Peter sees you upset, he'll want to know why.

ANN: We can't do this to him. I won't let you put him in one of those places.

DAILEY: It's not as bad as it sounds. I've seen the facilities. They're very clean and modern. I'm sure Uncle Peter will be happy there.

ANN: He's happy here.

DAILEY: He only seems happy. His condition has been getting worse every day. We've all been hoping that Uncle Peter would get better without the need for full time professional help, but that just isn't going to happen.

He needs medical help. Phil is having him consigned to a hospital run by a Dr. Reid. Reid is one of the top men in the profession.

ANN: Dr. Reid. I've heard of him somewhere. I think it was on the news. Something about his methods.

DAILEY: His methods are revolutionary. He's one of the most sought after doctors in the country.

ANN: I don't care about all that. We can't lock Peter up.

DAILEY: Mother, listen to me. Dr. Reid reviewed the tapes of Uncle Peter's sessions with Dr. Bates. He said that without treatment, Uncle Peter's condition will probably deteriorate. If we wait too long, he may become incurable.

Ann sits down. She is overcome with emotion. Dailey sits and puts his arm around her.

ANN: How long would he have to stay there?

DAILEY: That's impossible to say.

ANN: Would we be able to visit him?

DAILEY: I'm sure we would.

Koestler appears on the porch. He is whistling a lively tune as he enters.

KOESTLER: Hello, Jack. You're home a little early, aren't you?

DAILEY: A little.

KOESTLER: That's good. You've been working too hard lately.

He goes to the bookcase, chooses a book, then sits in one of the chairs.

DAILEY: You aren't planning on going out again, are you, Uncle?

KOESTLER: Not unless something comes up. Why?

DAILEY: I was just wondering. We're going to be eating soon.

KOESTLER: Oh. Well, I don't think I'll be going anywhere.

He starts to read.

ANN (*uncertainly*): Peter . . .

KOESTLER: Yes?

Dailey looks harshly at Ann.

ANN: Um . . . Peter . . . You know that anything I do, I do

for your own good, don't you?

KOESTLER (*gently*): I know. You shouldn't worry so much about me. I'm okay.

ANN (*to Dailey, almost desperately*): Jack . . .

DAILEY (*quickly*): Mother, you don't look well. You had better go up and take some of your medicine.

She hesitates, then exits. Pause.

KOESTLER: Compassion isn't necessarily an illness, Jack.

DAILEY: You grow tiring, Uncle.

(*Pause*)

KOESTLER: Jack, it kills her to see us fight with each other. Why don't we try to be friends? We should do things together.

DAILEY: Like what?

KOESTLER: We could go out to the lake and feed the ducks. It's very relaxing. When you're sitting out there at night, you feel such a sense of release. It would do you some good to sit back for once and enjoy just being alive.

DAILEY: I find life enjoyable enough without having to feed ducks.

KOESTLER: We still should try to be friends. It's not fair to Ann, being forced to watch us tear at each other.

DAILEY: Do you think it's fair that she has a brother she's ashamed to be seen with in public? Do you think it's fair that she has people point and whisper when she walks down the street?

KOESTLER (*sadly, to himself*): They just don't understand.

DAILEY: Well, neither do I.

A knock is heard at the door. Dailey admits Harry.

HARRY: Hello, I was sent by Dr. Reid. I'm looking for Peter Koestler.

DAILEY: That's him.

KOESTLER: What is this?

Harry grabs him. He struggles. Harry holds him in an armlock.

KOESTLER: Jack, what's going on?

DAILEY: We're having you committed to a mental hospital.

KOESTLER: You can't do that. Does Ann know about this?

DAILEY: She knows.

HARRY: Look, are you going to make trouble?

KOESTLER (*quietly*): No. No trouble. Can I pack some things?

HARRY: They didn't say anything about that. I'm just supposed to bring you to the hospital.

DAILEY: I'll have Mother pack for you. We'll come by the hospital later on.

HARRY: Okay, let's go.

DAILEY: Hey, you don't have to hold him like that. He said he won't cause any trouble.

HARRY: How do I know he won't make a break for it?

Pause. Dailey looks at Peter with respect.

DAILEY: Because he said so. (*Harry lets him go.*) Goodbye, Uncle Peter.

Koestler exits, followed by Harry. Dailey goes to the door and watches them leave. Lights dim.

Curtain

ACT TWO

Scene One

A room in Dr. Reid's sanitarium. There are two single beds, a couple of chairs, and a table with a potted plant. There is a door at stage right and a window with bars at stage left. As the scene opens, Nigel is sitting on one of the beds, his legs pulled up to his chest. Enter Koestler, led by Nurse Opel.

OPEL: This is where you will be staying, Mr. Koestler. This is Mr. Tonn, your roommate.

KOESTLER (*to Nigel*): Hello.

OPEL: Let me know if you need anything. Harry will be coming in shortly to administer some tests.

KOESTLER: Harry. Is he that big, beefy fellah who brought me over here? (*Opel nods.*) Is he a typical example of the staff here?

OPEL: How do you mean?

KOESTLER: I mean he was obviously hired more for his size than his intellect.

OPEL: I wouldn't know.

KOESTLER: Hey, loosen up. I don't bite. (*Starts to sit down, then an idea occurs to him.*) Oh, maybe sometimes.

He leaps for Nurse Opel and makes loud chewing noises as he pretends to eat her shoulder.

OPEL (*shocked*): Mr. Koestler, stop! (*She struggles with him, then begins to laugh.*) Mr. Koestler, stop it. What if Dr. Reid came in? (*Koestler chews his way over her shoulder and starts down her back. As a last resort, she plays along.*) Down, boy. Down! (*Koestler drops to his knees in a begging dog pose. Nurse Opel is amused.*) I can tell you're going to be a handful.

KOESTLER: If I'm lucky.

He starts to rise.

OPEL (*as a benevolent warning*): Down boy.

He leans back against the table.

KOESTLER: I think I'm going to like it here.

OPEL: I need to be getting on with my duties. Are you going to behave yourself?

KOESTLER: Scout's honor.

OPEL: Okay. Harry will be in soon. Then dinner will be served in the room at six.

KOESTLER: I've already had mine, thank you. (*Opel*

smiles, slightly flustered, then starts to exit.) Wait. You haven't told me your name.

OPEL: I'm Ms. Opel.

KOESTLER: I know that. What's your first name?

OPEL: Sharon.

She exits. Koestler turns to Nigel.

KOESTLER: Well, it looks as though we're going to be rooming together. My name is Peter. (*He offers his hand, but it is refused.*) Been here long? (*Pause*) I just got in today. (*Pause*) It looks like a nice place. (*smiles*) Pretty nurses. (*Pause*) This is supposed to be a good hospital. I hear they're very modern. (*Nigel looks up abruptly.*) I hear Dr. Reid is one of the best in his field. (*Pause*) I've been to a lot of psychiatrists. None has ever been able to cure me, though. (*under his breath*) As if that's what I wanted.

NIGEL (*intensely interested*): Don't you want to be cured?

KOESTLER: Not especially.

NIGEL: He'll do it. Dr. Reid can cure anybody.

KOESTLER: Is he helping you? (*Nigel turns his back and clams up again.*) Do you like Dr. Reid? (*Long pause*) I know this is kind of strange for both of us. Maybe we can help each other through it. Like when things start confusing us, when there are things we don't understand, we can talk about it and maybe we can figure it out together.

Nigel looks at him desperately.

NIGEL: Do you get lonely sometimes?

KOESTLER: Often.

NIGEL: Me, too. (*He thinks for a moment, then speaks desperately.*) Why do they want us cured?

KOESTLER: They think it will help us.

NIGEL: Don't they know how much it hurts?

KOESTLER: They think it will be worth it.

NIGEL (*pulls legs up and sulks*): They don't have to be in here.

(*Pause*)

KOESTLER: How long have you been here?

NIGEL: Six months. Seven. I'm not sure. How about you? Is this your first time in a place like this?

KOESTLER: Yes.

NIGEL: What were you put in here for?

KOESTLER: I have strange ideas. For instance . . . (*He steps up to the potted plant.*) I have a theory about plants. I think it was plants that were created in God's image, rather than people. Plants never fight, never go to war, and they are bursting with life. They stretch their leaves up to the sky and reach their roots down into the ground, gaining nourishment from God's soil and sunlight.

NIGEL: Then what are people for?

KOESTLER: People are just fertilizer producing machines. We're supposed to eat the other animals and produce fertilizer to help nourish the plants. That's why the world is in such bad shape now. We're being punished for not fulfilling our destiny. Instead of allowing our fertilizer to drop on the soil, we flush it into the sewer. That is our greatest sin. That, coupled with the fact that . . . (*Motions to the potted plant.*) . . . some people keep plants in slavery.

NIGEL (*laughs*): You *are* crazy.

KOESTLER (*smiling*): Thank you.

NIGEL (*smiles, timidly*): My name is Nigel.

KOESTLER: Pleased to meet you, Nigel.

NIGEL (*brightly*): I've got delusions.

KOESTLER (*laughs*): Don't we all?

Enter Harry, carrying a satchel.

HARRY: Dr. Reid told me to administer some test to you. My name is Harry.

KOESTLER: We met on the way over here, remember? I was being dragged, you were doing the dragging. (*Harry stands for a moment, at a loss for what to say.*) About these tests, Harry, why don't you just get my answers out of your files? I've taken them all a hundred times.

HARRY: Are you refusing to cooperate?

KOESTLER: I wouldn't dream of it. I always believe in cooperating. It's like I heard from this bumble bee the other day. I was over on Sixth Avenue when he came by and landed on my shoulder. I asked him how it is that bees are able to work in such harmony with each other, and he said—

HARRY: Wait a minute. I'm lost. You say you were talking to a bumble bee?

KOESTLER: Any reason why I shouldn't?

HARRY: Yes!

KOESTLER: Harry, you surprise me. I never would have taken you for a bigot.

HARRY: Is this a joke?

KOESTLER: I don't think it's a joking matter when you refuse to talk to someone just because they're different from you.

HARRY: But a bumble bee? You mean an actual little bee that flies around and has a stinger and everything?

KOESTLER: At least the bee carries his stinger out where everyone can see it.

HARRY: All of this seem to be beside the point. Let's get on with these tests.

KOESTLER: Sure.

HARRY: First, we're going to do word association. I'll say a word, and you say the first word that comes into your mind. All right?

KOESTLER: All wrong.

HARRY: No, don't start.

KOESTLER: Yes, do stop.

HARRY: Stop that!

KOESTLER: Go this!

HARRY: Mr. Koestler!

KOESTLER: Harry!

HARRY: Settle down!

KOESTLER: Unsettle up!

Harry grabs Koestler's mouth and holds it securely.

HARRY: Now don't start until I'm ready. (*He lets go of Koestler's mouth and picks up his notebook. He starts to say something, but when he looks at Koestler's intent, eager expression, he changes his mind. Instead, he looks into the notebook and begins the test.*) Black.

KOESTLER: Night.

HARRY: Large.

KOESTLER: Small.

HARRY: Girl.

KOESTLER: Oboy!

Harry eyes him suspiciously, then continues.

HARRY: Money.

KOESTLER: Help.

HARRY: Push.

KOESTLER: Recede.

HARRY: Sex.

KOESTLER: Ms. Opel. (*Harry eyes him again. Nigel is grinning. Koestler suddenly looks shocked and leans forward as if he is looking intently at something. Harry strains to see it. Koestler looks up abruptly. Blurts—*) Boy!

HARRY (*responds automatically*): Girl.

KOESTLER: Shirt.

HARRY: Pants.

KOESTLER: Laugh.

HARRY: Cry.

KOESTLER: Strong.

HARRY: Weak.

KOESTLER: Watermelon pits.

Harry looks confused for a moment, then scowls.

HARRY: Wait a minute.

KOESTLER: Go an hour.

HARRY: Stop!

KOESTLER: Go!

Harry grabs Koestler's mouth again.

HARRY (*in awe*): Boy, this stuff can get outta hand if you're not careful. (*He lets go of Koestler's mouth.*) I think that's enough word association for today.

KOESTLER (*disappointed*): Awwww.

HARRY: Let's try the Rorschach test.

KOESTLER: Can Nigel play?

HARRY: No. I'm supposed to test you. (*Pulls out cards. Holds up first one.*) Now, what do you see?

KOESTLER: I see a small boy climbing up a hill to his grandmother's house in a roaring blizzard . . .

HARRY: Okay.

He starts to put the card away. Koestler grabs his arm.

KOESTLER: Wait. I'm not finished. I see the grandmother standing on her porch, peering through the blizzard, watching for her grandson through her feeble eyes. (*Harry begins to peer at the card, trying hard to see whatever Koestler sees.*) She's holding a scarf she knitted for him on long, cold evenings as she sat alone by the fireplace. I see his dog running faithfully by his side, eager to please his master in any way he can. I see the birds . . .

HARRY: That's enough. We have a lot more of these to look at. (*He pulls out the next card.*) Now, what do you see in this one?

KOESTLER: I see a small boy climbing up a hill to his grandmother's house in a roaring blizzard. I see the grandmother—

HARRY: Hey, wait a minute.

KOESTLER: What's wrong?

HARRY: I don't know. (*He looks at the two different cards, then looks at the stack they haven't seen yet.*) Probably not much sense looking at the rest of these. (*Scratches his head. Looks through his notes.*) I think I need another conference with Dr. Reid. Something went wrong. I'll be right back.

He exits. Nigel, who had been struggling to keep back his laughter, now lets go.

NIGEL: That was great. Did you see the look on his face?

KOESTLER: If Dr. Reid is anything like Harry, this place will be a cinch.

At the mention of Reid's name, Nigel freezes.

NIGEL: He's not. He's not like him at all. (*Nigel turns abruptly to Koestler.*) Maybe you shouldn't have done that. They're going to be mad.

KOESTLER: What can they do?

Nigel turns away and does not answer. Enter Nurse Opel carrying a tray with two meals.

OPEL: Are you gentlemen ready to eat?

KOESTLER: That depends. What's on the menu?

OPEL (*smiling*): Just what you see on the tray. (*She sets it down.*) I'll leave this here. You can call me when you're finished.

She turns to exit.

KOESTLER: Sharon? (*She stops and turns.*) Am I just here for tests, or does Reid have the authority to treat me?

OPEL: I'm not allowed to answer that.

KOESTLER: You just did. Thank you.

She waits a moment, then exits. Pause.

NIGEL: Dr. Reid can do anything he wants here.

KOESTLER (*smiles*): I'm sure your Dr. Reid is a very intelligent man, but I'll bet he doesn't know about angels.

NIGEL: What?

KOESTLER: Angels have wings.

Koestler pulls a plate to himself and begins to eat with enthusiasm. Nigel watches him. The lights quickly fade.

ACT TWO

Scene Two

Koestler's room in the asylum the next day. Nigel sits on his bed. Koestler crouches by the window, examining the lock.

NIGEL: What are you doing?

KOESTLER: I'm trying to figure out if I can work this lock. It's a little more complicated than the ones my friend taught me on, but the principle is the same. I'll need a bent piece of metal. When they bring our dinner, I'll see if one of the forks might work.

There is a pause while he continues to study the lock.

NIGEL: You'll get in trouble.

KOESTLER: I've been in trouble before.

NIGEL: Not with Dr. Reid.

KOESTLER: I'll take my chances.

(*Pause*)

NIGEL: Peter?

KOESTLER: What?

(*Pause*)

NIGEL (*quietly*): Don't leave me.

Koestler turns slowly, then moves to sit by him on the bed.

KOESTLER: I can't stay here. (*Nigel ducks his head sadly.*) Would you like to come with me?

NIGEL: Could I?

KOESTLER: Sure.

NIGEL: I promise I won't be any trouble. We can go anywhere you want. We can go far away where nobody else can come.

KOESTLER: Sure. We'll be okay.

Enter Reid and Harry.

REID: Hello, gentlemen. I hope you slept well. Nigel, if you will be so kind as to go with Harry, it's time for your treatment. Dr. Knowles will be assisting.

Nigel and Harry exit. Reid looks at Koestler.

REID: As I'm sure you've guessed by now, I'm Dr. Reid.

KOESTLER: Hello.

REID (*brightly*): Have you been getting settled in here all right?

KOESTLER: A bit.

REID: I want you to relax. Feel at home. We're very informal here. You and I will have several sessions together to get acquainted before we decide on a treatment.

KOESTLER: Before *we* decide?

REID: The patients choose their own treatment here. Based upon my observations, of course.

KOESTLER *(ironically):* Of course.

REID: So I want everything to meet with your approval. Are you comfortable here?

KOESTLER: Barbed wire fence, gorilla orderly—very impressive.

REID (*grins in spite of himself*): Harry told me you gave him quite a time.

KOESTLER: Never send a baboon to do an inquisitor's job.

REID: Do you resent being here?

KOESTLER: It's not so bad. (*He goes to the window and speaks grandly.*) Though the windows may have bars, I still can hear the stars.

REID: Tell me about that. What do the stars sound like to you?

KOESTLER: Hope.

REID: Hope?

KOESTLER: Yes. If you could take Hope and transform it into a sound, that's what the stars sound like.

REID: And what do you hope for?

KOESTLER: A world where Peter Koestler will not be considered insane.

REID: Which would be better? To change the world or to change one man?

KOESTLER: Is the man right?

REID: Suppose he just thinks he's right?

KOESTLER: Then he should be allowed to follow his star in peace. You asked me if I resent being here. I resent being condemned for my good traits and blessed for my bad. When I was a businessman, I was loved. Now that I'm an angel, I'm punished. I resent the fact that I'm in here and my nephew is out there.

REID: It's only natural that you should feel a certain animosity toward your nephew at this point.

KOESTLER: My nephew is only a victim himself.

REID: Then who is the enemy?

KOESTLER (*looks away and speaks slowly*): That, I haven't discovered yet. I only know that there's something wrong with a world that hounds me as though I were insane simply because I stopped seeing life as a battleground and began seeing it as a Paradise. (*Turns back to Reid.*) It's so rare to see a person actually follow the inner voice which tells them who they really are. And when one of these rare human beings comes along, one of the true individualists, the world tries to crush the life out of them.

REID: One of the rare human beings like yourself, for instance.

KOESTLER: Like myself, for instance. Or Nigel.

REID: When Nigel came here he was violent, even dangerous. As you can tell, the improvement has been remarkable. As for yourself, I understand you better than you realize. For instance, I know you don't really hear the stars.

Koestler sits and stares powerfully at him.

KOESTLER: Go on.

REID: All your life you regretted the fact that the stars don't sing, that there is no Santa Claus, that men don't have the benevolence of plants. In short, you have regretted that the world is not Paradise. You sought happiness in your intellectual and financial pursuits, but these were a poor substitute for Heaven. Then, after you gained financial security and could live any way you chose, you decided to live as if the world were a Paradise after all. You pretended to hear the stars, you pretended to talk to animals, and when people took you seriously, you were amused. You decided to take the game to its limit . . .

KOESTLER (*finishing the statement*): . . . and show people what it's like to be an angel in Paradise. But if you believe that . . .

REID: Then why did I allow you to be committed? I didn't just allow it. I pressed for it.

KOESTLER: Why?

REID: Because you really are insane.

KOESTLER (*in awe*): You really believe that, don't you?

REID: I do. Your insanity does not manifest itself in

hallucinations, but, rather, in your frenzied search for Paradise. You have definite delusions and acute monomania which compounds your condition and is very destructive to your emotional and psychological makeup. But don't worry. I can help you.

KOESTLER: I don't want your help. (*The door opens and Harry enters, helping Nigel into the room. Nigel is drenched in sweat, his hair matted to his head. His eyes are glazed and he can barely walk. Koestler jumps up.*) Nigel! (*Harry drags Nigel to his bed. Koestler rushes over. He pulls Nigel's eye open with his thumb and lets it snap back. He turns to Reid.*) What have you done to him?

REID: Sometimes the treatment hits them pretty hard. It'll wear off.

KOESTLER: Treatment?! What kind of treatment do you have here?

REID: You wouldn't understand it.

KOESTLER (*firm, almost vicious*): Try me.

REID: It's a variation of electrotherapy—

KOESTLER: Electrotherapy!?

REID: I know what you're thinking, but it's not like that at all. I use my own technique, based on the stimulation of the motivational centers of the brain. The desired thought processes are taught to the patient who is then stimulated if they stray from the desired behavioral and thought patterns.

KOESTLER: Brainwashing! That's all you're talking about. Brainwashing through torture! Shock them if they do wrong until their minds become putty.

REID: Calm down, Koestler. I knew you would not understand. These procedures might be termed brainwashing if they were used on normal individuals. Nigel is suffering from delusions which incite negative behavior patterns which must be eliminated.

KOESTLER: He's suffering from the treatments! (*He rises and moves menacingly toward Reid.*) You said he got violent? Well, if you ever hook that child up to your machine again, I'll show you what violence is!

Harry holds him back.

REID: Calm down, Mr. Koestler. (*steps to door*) Ms. Opel, come in here. (*She enters.*) Mr. Koestler needs some medication to calm him down. See to Mr. Tonn first, though.

OPEL: Yes, sir.

She goes to Nigel, checks his eyes, then begins to take his pulse.

REID (*to Harry*): Take him to my office.

KOESTLER (*being forced out of the room*): You remember what I said and keep your machines away from that boy.

Koestler and Harry exit.

REID (*to Opel*): I want you to rearrange the schedules. I'm afraid Mr. Koestler is going to have to undergo electrotherapy.

Lights fade.

ACT TWO

Scene Three

Same room in the asylum, two days later. Nigel is pacing. Koestler sits on the bed.

KOESTLER: You okay?

NIGEL (*abruptly, nervously*): Sure.

KOESTLER: Trust me.

Nigel stops pacing and looks at him.

NIGEL: I do. (*goes to window and stares out*) I can't see your star.

KOESTLER: It's out there.

NIGEL: I'll find it.

KOESTLER: Do you remember everything I told you?

NIGEL: Yes.

Enter Reid and Harry.

REID (*to Nigel*): It's time for your treatment. (*Nigel and Harry exit.*) And how are you today?

KOESTLER: Still captive.

REID: You'll live.

KOESTLER: Think so? When I was at the university I saw an experiment they did with two groups of rats. The experiment was conducted by a colleague of mine, Dr. David Lee. Every day he would pick up each rat in Group One and squeeze it until it hurt slightly, then let it wriggle free as if by its own effort. The rats in Group Two were squeezed with the same amount of pressure as those in Group One, but they were not allowed to wriggle free. After a few moments, they were put back in their cage. The rats in Group One remained strong and healthy. The rats in Group Two died within a matter of months. Dr. Lee concluded that a feeling of helplessness is physically disabling in and of itself. (*Walks to the window and stares out.*) I wonder whether any useful knowledge is to be gained by torturing small animals.

REID: Some animals are worthless.

KOESTLER (*turns to him slowly*): Is that your professional opinion? (*Pause*) How much would you assess Nigel's value at?

REID: All human beings are valuable. And redeemable. I'm not a monster, Dr. Koestler. I'm a dedicated medical professional. I'm good at what I do, and I'm proud of it. I only take special cases, those whose sole problem is that their thinking habits have strayed until their behavior is detrimental to their well-being. My patients show no sign of physical damage, no tissue degeneration, and yet their ability to function has deteriorated. I turn them into healthy, productive members of society.

KOESTLER: You amaze me. You commit torture and consider yourself noble.

REID: Sometimes what I do does resemble torture. You think I don't know the pain Nigel goes through? I suffer every time I have to give him a treatment. He's going through Hell at my hands, but I'll drive the sickness out of him if I have to burn down to his very soul.

KOESTLER: I see more clearly now who the enemy is.

Harry bursts into the room.

HARRY: Dr. Reid! Come quick!

REID: What is it?

HARRY: Mr. Tonn has escaped!

REID: What?!

HARRY: We hooked him up to the machine, but it wouldn't work, and while we were checking it, he took off.

REID: How did he get out of the straps?

HARRY: I don't know.

REID: Well, get after him! Catch him before he reaches the gate!

Harry exits.

KOESTLER: It appears the rat has escaped by his own effort.

REID (*turning to face him*): Where is he?

KOESTLER: Who?

REID: I don't have time to play games with you. We both know that he never would have escaped without your prompting, and never could have escaped without your help. You must have planned the whole thing for him.

KOESTLER: Really?

REID: You're not as smart as you think you are. He'll never get outside the gate. He wouldn't even have gotten this far if the machine hadn't broken down.

KOESTLER: That was a fortunate coincidence, wasn't it?

Reid's face lights up with realization.

REID (*quietly*): You bastard.

KOESTLER: Careful, doctor. You're losing your objectivity.

Harry rushes in.

HARRY: He's out.

REID: What do you mean?

HARRY: He cut a hole in the gate and escaped.

REID: Show me. (*Rushes to the door, then turns back.*) I'll talk to you shortly.

KOESTLER: I'll be here.

Exit Reid and Harry. They close the door. Koestler goes to the window, opens it, then picks the lock on the bars. He opens them, and Nigel climbs in.

NIGEL: It worked great! You should have seen the look on their faces when the machine broke down.

KOESTLER: Did you have any trouble with the straps?

NIGEL: Not a bit.

KOESTLER: Good. Now you'll have to wait about ten minutes before you can escape. They'll have someone guarding the hole in the fence, but every spare person will be out looking for you. You can cut a new hole, and you'll be free. Do you remember what you're supposed to do when you get out of here?

NIGEL *(as though reciting something memorized):* I'm supposed to go to Meadowlawn Avenue and find Officer Jameson. He's a cop, but he's okay.

KOESTLER: Right. He'll help you out. It might be a good idea for you to get out of town.

NIGEL: I wish I could go back to my family.

There is an awkward pause.

KOESTLER: You'd better be going. Reid will be back soon.

NIGEL *(somber):* This was supposed to be your escape.

KOESTLER: I can wait.

NIGEL: Please come with me.

KOESTLER: I can't. I've got to keep the doctor off balance until you get safely away.

NIGEL: You know what he'll do to you.

KOESTLER: I can take it. I'll wait a few days, then escape myself. Now go.

Nigel crawls out the window. Koestler relocks the bars, closes the window, and returns to the bed. He picks up a book and starts reading. Enter Reid.

REID: Are you going to tell me where he's gone?

KOESTLER: No.

Reid locks the door, then turns to Koestler.

REID (*firmly*): Now we begin.

Curtain

ACT THREE

Scene One

Scene opens in Dr. Reid's office. Three weeks have passed. Reid sits at his desk. He is reading a report as Nurse Opel enters.

OPEL: Excuse me, Doctor.

REID: Yes?

OPEL: Sergeant Beale just called. They've located Mr. Tonn.

REID (*excited*): Where was he?

OPEL: He was camping out at Lake Myers. He refused to say who was helping him.

REID: What are they going to do with him?

OPEL: They've agreed to return him here since there are no charges against him.

REID: Are they bringing him now?

OPEL: Yes, sir.

REID: Good.

OPEL: There's one more thing.

REID: Yes?

OPEL: Jack Dailey is in my office. He insists on seeing you.

Reid leans forward abruptly and scowls.

REID: He does? (*accusingly*) I suppose you wouldn't know what he wants to see me about?

OPEL: How do you mean?

REID: Their attorney called me at home last night.

OPEL (*guiltily*): Oh.

REID: Yes, "oh". Who authorized you to talk to him?

OPEL: Peter asked me to. They're old friends.

REID: Peter is it? Since when are you on a first name basis with our patients? (*pause*) Answer me.

OPEL: I only . . . I just . . .

REID: You just what? Frankly, Ms. Opel, your whole conduct has been unprofessional lately. You have allowed yourself to become personally involved with the patients. You have let your feelings hinder your judgement. Do you think you know as much about medicine as I do? Do you think you're qualified to treat these patients yourself?

OPEL: No, sir.

REID: I don't know what to do about you. You've spent so much time talking with Mr. Koestler that it has begun to affect your work. I admit he's a very persuasive man, but he's ill.

OPEL: Do you think the electrotherapy is helping him?

REID (*angrily*): You stand there not three feet away from me and miss every word that comes out of my mouth. I'll not have you questioning my medical decisions.

OPEL: Yes, sir.

REID: Now send in Mr. Dailey.

OPEL: Yes, sir.

She starts to exit, but he speaks.

REID: One more thing. If you ever discuss the treatment of a patient with someone outside this institution again, I'll take you before the medical board and have your license revoked.

OPEL: Yes, sir.

She exits. Enter Dailey.

REID: Hello, Mr. Dailey.

DAILEY: Hello.

REID: Please be seated. (*Dailey sits.*) I'm afraid you're wasting your time by coming here. It's like I told your attorney yesterday, it would be impossible to have your uncle released from here at this time.

DAILEY: That's not why I came. Maybe my uncle does need the treatments you're giving him—I'm no doctor—but I want to know why we're not allowed to see him.

REID: The success of these treatments depends upon his total isolation from any outside influence. If he were permitted to have contact with you and your mother, he might revert back to his former behavior patterns. We almost have him at the point where he can be helped, and I cannot risk contamination from the outside.

DAILEY: You don't understand. You can't cut him off from my mother. It's going to kill him. I agree my uncle is sick, but I didn't have him committed here as a permanent condition. I just wanted you to declare him incompetent so that he could not squander his fortune. He's not dangerous. He just needs to be taken care of.

REID: When you had him committed here, you made me responsible for him. No one leaves here while they're still sick.

DAILEY: I'm not asking that he leave here. All I'm asking is that you let us see him. Let Mother see him.

REID: Perhaps in a couple of weeks.

DAILEY: We haven't seen him in a month.

REID: That's my decision. I'm sorry. (*The intercom buzzes.*) Yes?

OPEL (*voice from intercom*): Mr. Tonn is here.

REID: Have Harry bring him in when Mr. Dailey leaves.

OPEL (*voice from intercom*): Yes, sir.

REID (*to Dailey*): If you will excuse me, I have to see a patient.

DAILEY (*rising*): I'll stay in touch.

REID: I assure you, there is nothing to be concerned about. The next time you see your uncle you will be amazed at the change.

DAILEY: Not too amazed, I trust.

There is a pause while they look at each other, then Dailey exits. Enter Harry and Nigel. Nigel is very frightened.

REID: Hello, Nigel.

NIGEL: Please don't hurt me.

REID: I won't. Sit down. Relax. You know we've all been very worried about you, Nigel. You never should have run off like that.

NIGEL: I'm sorry. I won't do it again. Peter made me. He made me do it. He's the one who messed up the machine and showed me how to get out of the straps.

REID: I am aware of Mr. Koestler's role in all of this; however, each of us is responsible for our own actions. Mr. Koestler prompted you, but you should have refused.

NIGEL: I didn't mean it. I'll do right. You'll see. I won't make any trouble anymore.

REID (*soothingly*): I know you won't. (*to Harry*) Take him to Room 104. (*to Nigel*) I'm giving you your own room now. You'll like that better, I think. (*to Harry*) Send Ms. Opel in on your way out.

HARRY: Yes, sir.

Harry and Nigel exit. Reid writes something on a slip of paper. Enter Opel. Reid hands her the paper.

REID: Give Nigel two capsules of this to help him sleep.

OPEL: Yes, sir.

She starts to exit.

REID: Wait. (*She turns*) Ms. Opel. Sharon. I'm sorry I spoke so harshly before. It's just that their attorney gave me such a hard time, and I've been under a lot of pressure with Nigel escaping and Koestler resisting treatment.

OPEL: I understand.

REID: How has Koestler been sleeping?

OPEL: Not very well. The night orderly said he paces for hours after lights out.

REID: That's a shame. It's so hard to get him to take any medication at all.

OPEL: I know.

(*Pause*)

REID: All right. You're excused.

Exit Opel. Reid rests his face in his hands as the lights slowly fade to black.

ACT THREE

Scene Two

Koestler's room in the asylum. It is the next day. The stage is dimly lit. Koestler is pacing. His face is haggard and he looks a great deal older. He keeps clasping his hands together to keep them from shaking. Enter Harry, carrying a tray of food.

HARRY: Time for lunch, Mr. Koestler. You better eat up. You're beginning to lose weight.

Harry sets down the tray and exits.

KOESTLER (*to himself*): Can't eat any of that. Probably drugged.

He begins pacing again. He suddenly gets an idea and goes to the window. He pulls a bent piece of wire from his pocket. His hand is shaking so badly that he drops it. He picks it up and begins to work on the lock. The trembling of his hands makes the task hopeless. He becomes frustrated and throws the wire down. Paces again. Enter Reid. Koestler cringes back. He is frightened but is trying to maintain his dignity.

REID (*quietly*): Hello, Peter. (*Koestler sits on the bed, pulls his legs up to his chest, and stares straight ahead.*) They found Nigel. (*Koestler turns abruptly.*) I've put him in another room. You have a bad influence on each other. (*Pause*) I promise you, everything will be all right once you stop fighting. It hurts for a long time while you're struggling, but one day you'll relax. Then you can begin to heal. (*Pause*) You know, the one thing I regret out of all this is that after you're cured, you'll hate me. I would have liked to have known you before your disorder. I think we might have been friends.

Pause, then Reid slowly rises and exits. Koestler begins pacing again. Enter Opel. Koestler rushes to her.

KOESTLER (*quickly*): Did you talk to Phil?

OPEL: Yes.

KOESTLER: And? What?

OPEL: He said that only Dr. Reid can authorize your release.

KOESTLER: Sharon, you've got to help me.

OPEL: That's why I'm here.

KOESTLER: Escape is no good. They'll just track me down. You've got to help me get released.

OPEL: If you can just convince Dr. Reid that you're better . . .

KOESTLER (*despairing*): It's no use. He's too sharp. I can't say I've stopped believing I'm an angel, because he never believed that anyway. (*He grabs her by the shoulders, talks quietly but intensely.*) Sharon, you've got to get me out of here. I'm ready to break. I know about brainwashing. I know what they want. There are certain steps they go through. Certain things they expect at each step. I've been trying to do things in the right order, each step of the process just ahead of him, but it's getting hard for me to remember what comes next. If you don't get me out of here soon, I'll crack.

OPEL: Just tell me what you want me to do, and I'll do it.

Koestler sits on the bed and clasps his head in his hands.

KOESTLER: I don't know. I don't know. I'm about to go crazy here alone. (*He looks up.*) Why doesn't Ann visit me? Why has she abandoned me here?

OPEL: She hasn't abandoned you. Dr. Reid thought it would be detrimental to your recovery for her to visit.

KOESTLER (*cynically*): Of course. We can't let her see what's happening. She might do the humane thing.

OPEL: Don't talk like that.

KOESTLER: Sorry. If I ever regain my sanity maybe I'll write a treatise on the direct correlation between torture and bitterness.

OPEL: Are you bitter? (*Koestler walks to the window, grips the bars, and rests his head wearily against them.*) You shouldn't be, you know. Everyone is just trying to help you.

Koestler lifts his head slowly.

KOESTLER: What?

OPEL: We just want what's best for you.

Koestler slowly turns to face her.

KOESTLER (*coldly*): Say that again.

OPEL: I'm saying this as a friend. Maybe you have to be broken down before you can be rebuilt.

KOESTLER (*quietly*): Get out.

OPEL: Peter . . .

KOESTLER: Get out!

OPEL: If only you would . . .

KOESTLER: Get out of here and don't come back!

Koestler grabs her by the collar and forces her toward the door.

OPEL: Peter! Wait!

KOESTLER: Am I going to have to hurt you?! Is that all

you people understand?! What's wrong with being an angel?! What's wrong with being happy?! (*Harry rushes in and pulls Koestler off of Opel. She starts to leave. Koestler shouts at her.*) You tell Reid something for me! You tell him he won't break me down! No matter what he does, he won't break me down! (*Opel exits. Koestler pulls free from Harry and stands there, staring at him. Convinced the crisis is over, Harry exits. Koestler paces again, then goes and sits by the window.*) I'm going to come through this. I've got to plan everything out. First, I have to escape. Then I can . . . (*He stops talking as he seems to realize something. He leans toward the window. He strains as though listening carefully. His voice is incredulous—*) I can't hear it anymore. (*Louder, frightened.*) I can't hear it anymore. (*He jumps up, grabs the bars, and shrieks.*) I can't hear it anymore!!!

Blackout

ACT THREE

Scene Three

Scene opens in the living room of Koestler's home, one month later. Ann sits watching the door. Enter Dailey, stage left, carrying a ledger. He is worn out and collapses into a chair.

ANN: Hard day?

DAILEY: The worst. Uncle Peter has been overloading us with work since he was released from the hospital. Says he has to make up for lost time. My department is way behind already. I'll probably have to work straight through the weekend to get these books up to date. He wants them first thing Monday morning.

ANN: Why don't you ask Peter for more time?

DAILEY: He'd never go for it. The only reason he's let me get this far behind is because I'm his nephew. Anyone else would be long gone by now.

Enter Koestler. His eyes are clear and alert. He is the picture of health. Dailey immediately begins to work in the ledger.

ANN: Hello, Peter. (*He grunts in reply.*) Supper will be ready soon.

KOESTLER: I'm not hungry. I have work to do.

ANN: You're going to have to stop pushing yourself so hard. You're liable to work yourself into a breakdown. (*Koestler looks up but says nothing.*) You got some mail. It's on your dresser.

Koestler exits, stage right.

DAILEY: Why did you say that about a breakdown?

ANN: I wasn't thinking.

DAILEY: You've got to be careful what you say around him now. Anything can set him off. He fired Mr. Sheffield today.

ANN: *Old* Mr. Sheffield?

DAILEY: That's the one.

ANN: Why?

DAILEY: No reason. Just came in and told him to clean out his desk. Said it's his company, and he'll decide who works there and who doesn't.

ANN: Sheffield has been with the company since the beginning.

DAILEY: That's not all. He just got through designing some new equipment for us. He wants to take the plans with him, but Uncle Peter won't sign a release. Sheff said he's going to take legal action. It's no use, though. He was working for us when he designed those plans, so they belong to the company. Still, it was an ugly scene. You wouldn't believe how morale has dropped around that place.

There is a knock at the door. Dailey answers it. Enter Mr. Cross.

DAILEY: Hello.

CROSS: Good evening. Is Mr. Koestler at home?

DAILEY: Just a minute.

Dailey goes to the archway at stage right.

ANN: Won't you sit down?

CROSS: Thank you.

DAILEY (*calling out*): Uncle Peter! Someone to see you! (*to Cross*) He'll be right down.

ANN: Is my brother expecting you?

CROSS: No, but we've done business before. Your brother is a very generous man. (*Ann fidgets uncomfortably. Enter Koestler carrying some letters. Mr. Cross rises to greet him.*) Ah, Mr. Koestler. I'm not sure if you will remember me . . .

KOESTLER (*coldly*): Mr. Cross. What can I do for you?

CROSS: I've sent you several letters recently and gotten no reply.

KOESTLER: I've been ill.

CROSS: Ah. I expected it might be something like that. You must have made a good recovery. You're looking very well.

KOESTLER: It's kind of you to say so.

There is a brief awkward pause, then—

CROSS: Yes, well, what I dropped by for is, you remember when I came to see you a couple of months ago?

KOESTLER: I do.

CROSS: Well, there must have been some oversight, because we never received the check you promised us.

KOESTLER: There was no oversight. I don't intend to give you a check.

CROSS: I don't understand.

KOESTLER: I'm not giving you any money.

CROSS: But your money would help feed so many people.

KOESTLER: I'm no longer interested in feeding people. If they want to eat, let them work. I'm through supporting moochers.

CROSS: But the families we help—

KOESTLER: Are no concern of mine. Good day, Mr. Cross. (*Cross hesitates as though considering what to say, then heads toward the door.*) And stop clogging my mailbox with pleas for money.

Exit Cross. Koestler locks the door, then sits on the couch next to Ann. He opens a letter and begins to read.

ANN: You were a little harsh.

Koestler looks up.

DAILEY: I think he was right, though. If he kept giving money away, he'd go broke.

KOESTLER: Interesting you should say that. *(He stares at Dailey, making him uncomfortable, then—)* I want you out of here by morning.

DAILEY: Uncle Peter!

ANN (*desperately*): Peter, don't do this. We're sorry we

sent you to that place. We didn't know what would happen to you.

KOESTLER: He did. Didn't you, Jack? Either way, this is your last night in the house. And you can leave your ledger behind. You won't need it at your new company.

DAILEY (*to Ann*): Mother . . .

KOESTLER (*barks*): Don't bring her into this! (*Pause*) You disgust me, Jack.

ANN: Peter, I can't let you—

KOESTLER: Quiet! This is no concern of yours.

(*Pause*)

DAILEY (*his voice quaking slightly*): I guess I'd better go pack.

KOESTLER: Just be careful what you take.

Dailey looks at his mother, then exits, stage right. Ann moves closer to Koestler on the couch. She puts her hand on his leg.

ANN: Peter, I want you to listen to me and try to understand. I love you. I always have. I loved you when you were crazy, and I even love you now, in spite of what you're doing. But I'm going to have to go with Jack. I know we've hurt you badly, and I'm sorry. There's nothing I can do about that now. Try and take care of yourself. Okay, Peter?

She kisses him on the cheek. He is virtually expressionless, but there are tears running down his face. Ann has tears in her eyes, also. She exits, stage right. Koestler sits in silence. Then we see the burglar from Act One, Scene One step up onto the porch. He tries the door, then the window. Since both are locked, he uses his tool on the door. Enters.

BURGLAR: Hey, Peter, how come your door's locked? It's still early.

KOESTLER: I always lock my doors now.

The burglar shrugs his shoulders and locks the door. Koestler goes to the desk which is downstage right and starts looking through the drawers. The burglar goes to the bar and begins to fix himself a drink.

BURGLAR: So where have you been lately? I keep coming by, but you're never here.

KOESTLER: I was in an asylum.

BURGLAR: Wow. That's too bad. I'm glad you're out. (*Koestler pulls a gun from the drawer and aims it at the burglar.*) What are you doing?

Koestler picks up the phone and dials.

KOESTLER: Hello, operator? Get me the police.

BURGLAR: Hey, what is this?

The burglar moves toward Koestler. Koestler brandishes the gun.

KOESTLER (*growls*): Hold it. (*The burglar stops.*) Hello, police? This is Dr. Peter Koestler of 1642 Meadowlawn. I have a prowler here. Would you please send a car in a hurry? Thank you.

He hangs up.

BURGLAR: What's wrong with you?

KOESTLER: They cured me.

BURGLAR (*quietly, with complete comprehension*): Oh, no.

The burglar starts to move toward the door.

KOESTLER: That's far enough. Don't make me shoot you. I will, you know.

BURGLAR: Peter, this is crazy.

KOESTLER: No. This is sane.

BURGLAR: Peter, step over to the window and listen. Your star is singing beautifully tonight.

KOESTLER: I never hear the stars anymore.

(Pause)

BURGLAR (*quietly*): I wish I had known they had you in there.

KOESTLER: It's just as well this way. (*Pause. The burglar begins looking around.*) Don't try anything. We're going to wait quietly for the police.

BURGLAR: Peter, let's go away from here. It's your family that caused your troubles. Come with me, and we'll go camp out under the stars. (*Pause*) They really did cure you, didn't they? Well, there's no way I could handle prison. If you're going to shoot me, it will have to be in the back, because I'm walking out that door.

KOESTLER: Don't do it. I swear I'll kill you.

BURGLAR (*ignoring this statement*): If you change your mind about coming with me, I'll be at Ted's on Eighteenth Street. (*smiles*) Ask for Jim. Everyone knows me.

He starts toward the door. Koestler aims at him, then his gun arm falls limply to his side. He reaches out his left hand, palm up, as though he were a beggar seeking alms. His voice is very strained and quiet, like a moan of pain.

KOESTLER: Jim . . . (*His pained expression shows his inner struggle for just a moment before his face turns hard. Suddenly, he swings the gun up, aims, and fires two loud blasts into Jim's back. Jim falls dead on the floor. Koestler speaks, his voice hard, cruel like we have never heard it before.*) When they cure you by torture, you stay cured.

Lights fade to black as Koestler stands there, watching the body. His expression never softens.

Curtain

SWAN SONG

A Play in One Final Act

Scene One

A bomb siren blares in the darkness. Lights come up on a small underground bomb shelter filled with crates and boxes, some open, some not. Against one wall is a bookcase filled with volumes on history, philosophy, literature, science. A short bench with no back rests in the center of the shelter. At the back wall is a ladder which leads to a hatch to the outside world. There is a radiation gauge on the wall and a radio on one of the crates.

Steve is alone in the shelter. He paces nervously, checking his watch from time to time. Ed appears at the top of the ladder and starts to descend; he is followed closely by Janet. Ed is forty-five, stocky, but trim for his age; powerful looking. Janet's features are sharp, well defined; her features show intelligence, independence, and just a trace of boredom.

The siren continues through the opening lines and must be shouted over.

ED: Where is everybody?

STEVE: You're the first.

ED (*checks watch*): They'll have to hurry. (*Enter Wendy, an attractive girl of twenty-three. She stumbles slightly on the ladder and is assisted by Ed.*) You okay?

She smiles and nods, then sits on the bench. Steve and Ed wait by the ladder. Janet leans against the wall, hands in her pockets. Enter Adam. He is probably in his late thirties or early forties, yet possesses a vivacity one would expect in a much younger man. Rather than descend the ladder one rung at a time, he wraps his arms and legs around it and slides down.

STEVE: Time is almost up.

ED: Better go ahead and bolt it.

STEVE: What about James?

ED: You know the rule. It's time to bolt it. Did you close the outer door, Adam?

Adam nods. Steve climbs up and closes the hatch, which cuts down on the noise of the siren. He bolts the door, then descends. The siren stops altogether. Adam jumps up on the bench.

ADAM: I suppose you're all wondering why I've asked you here today?

He is greeted with a few grins.

ED: Anyone want to play gin? I remembered a deck of cards this time. (*No one answers. He begins playing solitaire on the bench.*) What I want to know is, where do they get off throwing an unscheduled alert at us like this? It's really a hassle having to come all the way over here.

WENDY (*smiles*): It's only a couple of blocks. (*She pokes him in the stomach.*) The exercise is good for you.

ED (*laughing*): I guess you're right. And it's probably a good idea to keep us on our toes.

ADAM: At least we don't have to sit around doing nothing. I see Steve has brought those books down here. (*He goes to the bookcase. Steve joins him.*) Aristotle . . . Darwin . . . Shakespeare . . . This is quite a collection.

STEVE (*proudly*): I hope to bring a lot more down here before I'm finished.

Adam pulls out a volume and thumbs through it.

ADAM: These must be pretty expensive.

STEVE: Don't worry. I'm paying for it out of my own pocket. None of the money came from our fund.

WENDY: Why don't we use some of the money to get some comfortable chairs? This bench is murder.

STEVE: It's too crowded down here for any furniture. Besides, there are other things we need first. We haven't even bought any cots yet.

WENDY: We ought to make the shelter bigger.

ADAM: We can't afford it.

WENDY: We can't afford anything. (*She turns to Steve.*) Sometimes I wish we had never let you talk us into building this shelter.

JANET: I'd rather be in here than pressed into some Junior High School basement with fifty strangers.

WENDY: They never should have made it a law. People shouldn't have to go to shelters if they don't want to.

STEVE: I know it seems hard now, but, believe me, it's worth it. We're a lot safer in here than in one of those public shelters. It'll really pay off if we're actually attacked.

ADAM (*brightly*): Then I sure hope we get attacked. I'd hate to think we were wasting our money.

ED (*confidently*): There's not a nation in the world with enough guts to attack us. We're too powerful. I sleep peacefully at night knowing we've got enough nuclear warheads to blast the rest of the world into oblivion.

ADAM: I wish I had your outlook.

WENDY (*squirming*): I just wish I had a pillow. (*sweetly*) Steve, would you get me something to sit on?

STEVE: Sure. There must be something around here.

Steve digs through one of the crates.

WENDY: They always make us wait so long. (*She pulls a compact out of her purse and starts touching up her makeup.*) Don't they know how boring it gets down here?

ED: It won't be much longer.

Steve pulls out a blanket.

STEVE: I'm afraid this is the best I can do, Wendy. We don't seem to have any cushions.

WENDY: This is fine. Thank you. (*She settles herself like a hen over an egg.*) James was smart. Next time I think I'll stay home, too.

ED: And pay a nice fat fine if you get caught. These aren't just games we're playing here. The government has us do these alerts to prepare us for the real thing.

ADAM: That's awfully nice of them.

WENDY (*grumbling*): Just because someone invaded Belharain. Whoever heard of Belharain before? Did you? Now one nation invades, another sends aid, and suddenly it's the most important nation in the world.

ED: It's important because of what it represents.

ADAM: What it represents? Belharain is a desolate

wasteland. What could we or anyone else possibly want with it? I'll bet even the Belharainians don't want it.

ED: Its importance is strategic. Belharain is a militaristically vital crossroads.

ADAM: I know. I read the same editorial you did.

ED *(fuming):* It's also important as a signal that we're ready to stand and fight.

JANET: You mean 'kill.'

ED: What?

JANET: You said 'fight.' I was correcting your verb choice.

ED: Fight, kill, it's the same thing. The point is, we've got to show that we're ready to go all the way with this thing. That's why my plant got those government contracts. That's why we're gearing up for the production of war materials. We can't afford to show any weakness.

ADAM: Why not?

ED: Because our enemies would walk all over us. Haven't you got any patriotism?

ADAM (*evenly*): None at all.

ED (*contemptuously*): You were never in the service, were you, Adam?

ADAM: Nope. Never was.

ED: That explains it. If you had helped defend this country, you would feel more of the pride. My family has always done our part. I served three years in the Marines, and my boy laid down his life fighting for the supremacy of his country.

ADAM (*sadly*): I'll bet you were proud.

ED: Damn right I was. He died like a man. It burns me to see people sitting back smugly in the safety of their homes, belittling what our soldiers have done. Hell, if it weren't for the soldiers, they wouldn't have any homes to be sitting back smugly in. Freedom doesn't come easy. You have to fight for it. That's one thing the Founding Fathers understood when they set up this system. Sometimes a war is necessary for the good of the country.

STEVE: Not all of the Founding Fathers believed that.

ED: Name one who didn't.

STEVE: Benjamin Franklin. He said there never was a good war or a bad peace.

ED: He did not.

STEVE: Yes, he did. (*He moves to the bookcase.*) I think the quote is in Bartlett's.

ED: Show me.

Steve pulls out a book and turns to the index.

STEVE: Walls . . . Wants . . . War . . . (*He turns to somewhere near the end of the book and glances over the page.*) Here it is.

ED (*grumbles*): Hmmmm. (*He suddenly brightens.*) Aha! Listen to what George Washington said. Quote: To be prepared for war is one of the most effectual means of preserving peace. . . . Hey, look, Plato is on my side, too.

ADAM: I'll see your Plato, and raise you a Balzac.

Ed slams the book shut.

ED: Isn't there anything you take seriously?

ADAM: Not yet.

Ed returns the book to the shelf.

ED: I wonder what your parents must have been like.

ADAM: You would have liked them. They were two of the most God fearing, patriotic, war supporting people you could ever hope to meet.

ED: It's amazing how different you are from my boy. He was a fine Christian and a brave soldier.

ADAM (*ironically*): Onward Christian Soldiers . . . marching off to war.

ED: That's blasphemous.

ADAM: Isn't it.

STEVE: Let's find something else to talk about.

ED: That's fine with me. I was just trying to make Adam realize that— (*The lights flicker, then dim out.*) What is this?

STEVE: Somebody got a match?

WENDY: I do. Here.

STEVE (*lighting the match*): There should be some candles in this crate. (*He finds them.*) Here we go. (*He lights the candle and steps to the back of the stage behind some of the crates.*) It should only take a minute to get the generator working. (*The lights flicker, then come on full. Everyone claps.*) That's better.

ADAM: I wonder what made them go out?

STEVE: It could be a failure at the plant. Let's check the radio.

JANET: If the power is out, they're going to have a hard time controlling the looting, with most of us down in these shelters.

Steve turns on the radio and moves the dial. All we hear is static as the dial slowly moves across the numbers.

STEVE: I can't seem to get anything.

ED: Maybe there's a radio silence because of the alert.

ADAM: Try the Hadley station. It should be about 1180.

Steve tries.

STEVE: Nothing.

JANET: That doesn't make sense. Hadley never has alerts on the same days we do.

Steve continues to turn the knob. The static suddenly becomes louder, then we hear a voice.

ANNOUNCER: . . . tuned to this Emergency Broadcast Station for further updates.

A popping noise is heard, then complete silence.

ED: What was that all about?

STEVE: I don't know.

ED: See if you can get it again.

STEVE (*trying*): I can't. It's dead.

ADAM (*to himself*): Radio silence . . . Blackout . . .

ED: This must be what they meant by an "accelerated program of readiness."

STEVE: They shouldn't just spring it on us like this.

ED: They're trying to simulate the real thing.

STEVE: But a power blackout of the whole area can be dangerous.

WENDY: What do we do now?

ED: Wait for instructions.

ADAM: Like any well trained animal.

WENDY: What if they don't . . .

STEVE: Just a minute.

The radio is emitting a low-pitched whistle. This stops, and the Announcer begins.

ANNOUNCER: Attention . . . attention . . . All civilian vehicles must be kept off the streets. Repeat: all civilian vehicles must be kept off the streets. Military and civil defense units must have the streets clear. Stay tuned to this Emergency Broadcast Station for further instructions.

Again there is a popping noise, followed by silence.

(*Pause*)

JANET (*a slight quake in her voice*): This is too real.

ED *(tries to sound upbeat, but is obviously nervous)* It has to be. Don't worry. They'll signal "all clear" any time now. Come on, Steve, let's play some cards to pass the time.

Steve doesn't answer him. Everyone stares at the radio.

(*Pause*)

ADAM (*cold tension in his voice*): It does make you think, though. They could really do it. These alerts could become real.

STEVE: Never.

ED: Steve's right. There's nothing to worry about.

Again, we hear the low whistle.

ANNOUNCER: Attention . . . attention . . . This is repeating an earlier statement. The President of the United States has announced that at 6:54 o'clock, Eastern

Standard Time, United States airspace was violated by enemy warplanes. This is not an alert. Repeat: this is not an alert.

STEVE (*quietly, but with great fear*): Nooo . . .

ANNOUNCER: Retaliatory measures are being taken. There is no need for panic. Everyone must remain in their shelters. It is crucial that the streets be kept clear for military and civil defense vehicles. Stay tuned to this Emergency Broadcast Station for further instructions.

Pop, then silence. Ed is frozen, staring at the radio. He seems to be in panic. Adam and Steve also stare at the radio; Steve with fear and disbelief, Adam with fear and sadness. Janet stares tragically at Adam. Wendy keeps looking back and forth at all the others.

WENDY: What's going to happen? What does it mean?

JANET (*bitterly, close to tears*) It means we're at war! First hand!

The Announcer's voice suddenly comes shouting out of the radio without the prior warning tone.

ANNOUNCER: Attention! Attention! If this station discontinues broadcasting, tune to 1640 or—

He is cut off by deafening static, followed by silence.

STEVE: What happened?

Adam jumps to the radio and turns the dial.

ADAM: 1640 is dead, too. (*He turns the knob back and forth.*) There's nothing anywhere.

He continues to work the dial.

JANET (*quietly, tremulously*): They were hit.

WENDY: What?

JANET (*still quietly, almost in awe*): They're dead.

ED: They can't be. The military shelters are the best there are.

ADAM: They won't withstand a direct hit. The military targets—

The sound of an explosion cuts him off. Everyone looks up. There is another blast, followed by a low rumbling, like thunder. It continues for several moments.

WENDY (*shrieking*): Nooo!

She lunges for the ladder. Adam grabs her.

ADAM: It's too late.

WENDY: They can't!

Blast. Rumble.

JANET (*bitterly*): They did.

Three blasts. Rumble. Everyone moves closer together.

ED: We're safe down here, aren't we?

(*Pause*)

STEVE: James. He didn't make it.

WENDY: We don't know that. He might have gone to another shelter somewhere.

STEVE: No. We all knew to meet here. He wouldn't have gone anywhere else.

WENDY: Maybe he was out of town. You can't know for sure.

JANET: If he had come late . . .

STEVE: What?

JANET: Would we have heard him knocking on the hatch?

STEVE: I don't know.

ADAM: We should have left the door open longer.

ED: Then we'd all be dead.

WENDY (*almost hysterical*): He's not dead! He got safely to another shelter somewhere! I know he did!

STEVE (*holding her*): Okay, okay. Calm down. We can't afford to lose control. We've got to keep organized. Ed, check the radiation gauge.

ED: It's clear. No radiation at all. (*He turns his eyes toward the hatch.*) I wonder what it looks like up there.

JANET: Wasteland. Flat and barren.

Wendy's sobs magnify.

STEVE: (*to Janet*) Keep it down. (*to Wendy*) It's okay. Don't worry. Everything will be all right.

JANET: Why tell her that?

STEVE: Because it's true. They used conventional weapons. That means rescue teams can start flying in as soon as they get organized.

JANET (*bitterly*): Terrific. The Red Cross will fly in and return us home. Each to our own separate crater.

ED: It's not as black as you're making out. They're prepared for this sort of thing.

STEVE (*begins to pace*): Exactly. If we keep our heads and don't panic, we'll come out of this alive. (*As Steve talks, Wendy begins to calm down and eventually stops crying altogether.*) The people who survive this will be the ones who plan everything out. We'll have to stay underground for a while until we're sure the bombing is over. That means we had better set up a system of rationing.

ADAM: How much food have we got?

STEVE: Enough to last about two weeks. More if we're careful. Our water should last about that long, too.

ED: Is that figuring with or without James? (*There is a long, awkward pause. Ed begins to feel uneasy.*) Look, so we survived, and he didn't. That means there's more for us. . . . Come on, that's just a fact of nature. . . . Some survive, some don't. It's not our fault James is dead.

JANET: Why don't you shut up?

(*Pause*)

ADAM (*quietly*): That's a good idea about rationing, Steve. You want to handle it each day?

STEVE: Okay.

ADAM: What other provisions do we have?

STEVE: Bedrolls, blankets, some rope, various tools . . .

JANET: Do we have a stove?

STEVE: No, but we really don't need one. Most of our food doesn't require cooking.

JANET: Like what?

STEVE: Beans . . . dehydrated beef . . .

ED: Haven't we got anything decent?

ADAM (*lightly*): Where's your spirit of adventure, Ed? Pretend you're camping out. (*suddenly serious*) Better yet, pretend you're a Christian Soldier, roughing it in the trenches.

Ed gives Adam a hard look but decides to let the statement pass. Suddenly a high-pitched beeping noise is heard. Steve freezes, and his head jerks in the direction of the radiation gauge.

Everyone else looks around confused, except Adam, who looks at Steve, then follows his gaze to the gauge. Adam looks sad but calm.

ED: What is it?

STEVE: The gauge!

WENDY: What's wrong?

STEVE: It's into the danger zone! They used nuclear weapons! They bombed us with nuclear bombs!!!

Steve can no longer stand. He slumps to a sitting position on one of the crates.

ED: That's impossible! There was no radiation before!

JANET (*bitterly, savagely*): Of course not. You think they would waste nuclear bombs on us? We're getting the fallout from the big cities.

STEVE (*in awe*): What are we going to do? What is there to do? It's over. It's all over.

WENDY: Nooo!

Blackout

Scene Two

Same scene as before. Adam is crouched by the radio, trying the dial first one way, then the other. Steve is sitting on one of the crates, gazing ahead in a stupor. Janet is quiet, contemplative. Wendy is nervous and jittery. Ed is pacing, obviously frightened, but trying to quell the fear through nervous activity. Suddenly he stops and turns to Adam.

ED: When are you going to give it up? You've been trying that thing for hours. (*Adam continues to work in silence. Ed resumes pacing.*) Just because they used nuclear weapons, that doesn't mean everybody's dead, does it? Maybe there are whole parts of the world untouched.

JANET (*to Adam, as though she knows the answer*): Did you try the shortwave frequencies? (*Adam nods.*) Did you get a response? From anywhere in the world?

Adam does not answer. He just lowers his head until his forehead rests on the radio. After a moment, he raises his head.

ADAM (*to Ed, somber*): You were right about the wisdom of our government, though. They finally found the solution to war.

JANET: You just annihilate everybody.

STEVE: I can't believe God would let this happen. All our accomplishments, everything we built; it's all gone now.

JANET: Maybe God doesn't care about the accomplishments.

STEVE: Then what was it all for?

Ed drops to his knees next to the crate where Steve is sitting.

ED: Think, Steve! There must be something we can do. We can't just sit down here and die! What can we do, Steve?

STEVE (*in a stupor*): I don't know. . . . Nothing. . . . We've got a couple of weeks to live. A couple of weeks.

ED: No, Steve. No!

STEVE: Then our food will run out.

ED: We've got to do something!

Adam pulls a can of beans from one of the crates and tosses it to Ed.

ADAM *(bitterly):* Plant this. Maybe we can grow some canned goods.

STEVE: Wait! That's it! Why didn't I think of it before? (*He jumps up and grabs Adam by both sides of the head.*) Adam, you've done it! You've saved us!

He pulls Adam close and kisses him on the cheek.

ED (*frightened*): Pin him down! He's gone mad!

Steve lets go of Adam and turns to Ed, who cringes back.

STEVE: No, Ed. I haven't gone mad. Listen, we do have a chance. We're just getting fallout from other cities. It'll clear soon, and we can go out and plant crops.

JANET: What'll we use for seeds?

STEVE: We can find a store somewhere that's not hit too badly. Dig through rubble if we have to.

ED (*dawning on him*): It'll work. We can do it. We can do it. (*He hugs Steve. Wendy, who has been in shock up to now, joins them. Janet, somewhat reluctantly, does also. Only Adam remains apart.*) What's wrong with you?

ADAM (*as though thinking of something else*): Nothing. It sounds like a great idea.

Everyone releases each other as Steve talks.

STEVE: We'll have to find some undamaged ground to plant in, but that shouldn't be too difficult. We can go out into the country somewhere.

ED: What if other people get the same idea we did. What if they try to take our food? It can get pretty nasty.

STEVE: I hadn't thought of that. We'll have to arm

ourselves.

ED: If we find the right materials, I can construct a crossbow.

STEVE: That may not be enough. I wish we had a gun.

JANET (*amazed*): You people are sick. "I wish we had a gun." Darwin had the right idea, only in reverse. The Descent of Man. We started as apes and descended to this. Any justification God needed for all this, you just supplied.

ADAM: Calm down, Janet.

JANET: But you heard them. The whole world is destroyed, we have one small hope of survival, and their first thought is: "I wish we had a gun."

ADAM (*soothing*): Calm down. It's not important.

JANET: But, Adam—

ADAM: They're going to get what they deserve.

JANET: What do you mean?

ADAM: Something they didn't think of.

JANET: What's that?

ADAM: You can't grow crops in just two weeks. (*There is a pause while everyone stares at Adam. He continues slowly.*) Even if the fallout were to clear up enough so that we could go out safely, and even if the radiation were to wash out of the soil so that crops could grow, we would all be dead of starvation before we had enough grown to feed us. This hole we dug is our grave.

WENDY: Our grave?

ADAM: Yes. We're down here for the duration. We'll sit around hungry for a while, then we'll start to consider each other as possible meals.

STEVE: Adam!

ADAM: It's inevitable. We're going to start eating each other. In fact . . . (*suddenly cheerful*) . . . we will probably begin with Ed here.

ED (*jumps up*): This is intolerable!

STEVE (*quickly*): Calm down.

ED: He's going to far! He's sick! Let's throw him out of here!

WENDY: We can't do that.

STEVE: Don't be stupid, Ed. He's just letting off steam. He doesn't mean what he says.

ADAM: I don't? I naturally assumed Ed would be our choice. Who do you think we should eat first?

STEVE: Shut up!

ADAM (*bows grandly*): I beg your pardon.

He goes over to one of the crates and sits down. Everyone sits in dismal silence for a few moments before Wendy speaks.

WENDY: Is he right? Is there really not enough time to grow crops before our food runs out?

STEVE (*tired, unconvincing*): Sure there is. There's plenty of time.

WENDY: Our food will last two weeks?

ED: That's right.

WENDY: And how long does it take for crops to grow?

Her question echoes hollowly in a dead silence. Pause. Then Adam stands up and addresses the group with enthusiasm—

ADAM: Where's your sense of humor? We're sitting right in the middle of the grandest practical joke the human race has ever played on itself—its own extinction.

ED (*stands up, moves menacingly toward Adam*): If you don't shut up, I'll lay you out.

ADAM (*puffs out his chest with mock bravado*): Would you care to step outside?

STEVE: In the name of decency, why can't you shut up? The world has been blown to bits. There were billions of people alive just a short time ago. Now they're all piles of ash.

ADAM: Which means they've been put out of their misery. We should be celebrating. There's an idea! Let's have a party!

WENDY *(disgusted):* Adam!

ADAM: No, seriously. An "End of the World Party." The first annual "End of the World Party." (*He starts filling glasses with water from a barrel and passes them out.*) You'll see. We'll have a lot of fun. There's no reason not to, now. We have no responsibilities and nothing to do. (*He stops and holds his glass high in the air.*) I propose a toast: to the generals and the scientists, without whom none of this would have been possible.

Adam is the only one to drink. The others pour their water back into the barrel or set it aside, depending on where they are. Adam moves to the radio and turns it on.

STEVE: What are you doing now?

ADAM: Trying to find a dance station.

ED: Don't you have any decency at all?

ADAM: Apparently not. How about it, Wendy. Care to dance?

She turns away, repulsed.

ED: I swear, if you don't stop, I'll pound you. This is hard enough without your sick humor.

ADAM: I don't see why. We're going to be living through the same things, having the same things happen to us. You choose to be dismal. I choose to enjoy myself. We should learn a lesson from the swan. There's an animal that knows how to die. It goes out singing. Surely you would not begrudge me my swan song.

WENDY: But I don't want to die!

ADAM: Neither do I, but we've got no choice. What's the matter with you people? You're sitting around like a bunch of gargoyles. Ah, I know what the trouble is. You're dreading the canned beans. Not to worry. Old Adam has a solution to everything. We can go around to the stores that are left and gather up steaks, ribs; we can live like kings.

ED: Won't the meat have radiation poisoning?

ADAM: Certainly!

ED: You're insane!

ADAM: The world has been burned to a crisp by our scientists and leaders, the only humans alive are living underground like moles, we'll all die of starvation in a matter of weeks because our government could not afford to show any weakness, and you call me insane? Well, I'm going, whether anybody joins me or not.

JANET: If you go out there now, you'll be burned alive.

Adam checks the radiation gauge.

ADAM: The radiation levels are down. I'll be poisoned but not burned.

WENDY: When you open the door, the radiation will get down here.

ADAM: Not with the safety hatch.

JANET: The radiation poisoning will kill you eventually.

ADAM: Starvation will kill you. Maybe we can get together later and compare notes. Steve, you figure out my share of the ration, and I'll be going.

ED: If you use up your ration and come back here, we won't help you.

ADAM (*solemn*): I know. Steve, put my share in this bag.

He tosses him a burlap bag. While Steve fills it with cans of food, Adam puts a bedroll, eating utensils, etc., into a duffle bag. Janet goes over to him.

JANET: Will you be all right?

ADAM: Will you?

JANET: The radiation poisoning is going to hurt.

ADAM: If the pain gets too bad, I'll just go on top of a tall building and have a diving party. What will you do when the hunger gets to be too much? (*She turns and looks significantly at Ed. Adam laughs.*) Right. (*There is an awkward silence, then—*) Hey, I'll be fine. While everyone else is eating canned beans and dehydrated protein, I'll be dining on duck and pheasant. While they crouch in darkness, I'll walk tall in the sunlight.

JANET (*holding back tears with a smile*): King of the Dead World, eh?

ADAM: No. Not a king, exactly. A jester is more like it. (*He puts a burlap bag on his head in a comical way and begins to burlesque.*) I shall be . . . (*bows*) . . . Court Jester of the Dead World, spreading his Philosophy of Happy Doom from shelter to shelter. Can't you see it? There they'll be, sitting around in dismal little groups, waiting quietly for the end, and suddenly they will be confronted by . . . (*bows again*) . . . me! I daresay I'll shake them up a bit.

JANET (*laughs through the tears which now stream down her face*): And the lunatics shall inherit the Earth.

ADAM (*seriously*): No. They've owned it from the beginning. (*Smiles, spreads his arms grandly.*) Now it's my turn.

JANET: I'm going to miss you, Adam.

ADAM: Come with me, Janet. You don't want to sit around here. There's nothing to do but watch everyone grow thin. Come to my party.

JANET: I'm sorry. I just don't feel up to it.

ADAM (*sadly*): Understood. (*He kisses her hand, not in mockery, but with sincere respect. He looks at her for a second or two, then turns to the rest of the group.*) It's time for me to bid you all a fond adieu. Steve, have you got my food and water together?

STEVE: Right here.

ADAM: Thank you. Mind if I take some books along?

STEVE: Take any you want.

Adam chooses several and puts them into his duffle bag.

ADAM: You never know when you may need some kindling. And now, au revoir. (*He gives a loose salute and starts up the ladder, then begins to sing with great sentimentality—*) And the rockets' red glare, the bombs bursting in air . . . (*He turns to the others.*) Patriotic songs always make me feel warm all over.

As he ascends the ladder, the lights fade to black. Adam continues to whistle the Star Spangled Banner a few seconds in the dark. Then we hear the metallic sound of the slamming of the hatch.

Scene Three

Same scene as before. Two weeks have passed. The bench is now turned over on its side. Everyone is shabbier; they look fatigued. Wendy's forearm is wrapped in a piece of cloth. Janet is sitting on the floor at one end of the shelter, leaning back against a crate. Wendy is in a similar position at the other end of the shelter. Ed and Steve are between them, asleep on the floor. Wendy is fiddling with her wound under the bandage. She occasionally winces in pain.

JANET: Need some help?

WENDY: No.

JANET: You really should let someone take a look at that.

WENDY: I don't need your help!

JANET (*closing her eyes and leaning her head back*): Suit yourself.

Wendy start to cry silently. Ed stirs. Wendy, with extreme effort, holds back the tears.

ED (*sits up*): I'm hungry. (*He kicks Steve's feet.*) Steve, wake up.

STEVE (*not moving*): What is it?

ED: I'm hungry.

STEVE: You'll have to wait for ration.

ED: It's time.

STEVE: No, it's not.

(*Pause*)

ED: What gives you the right to hoard food?

STEVE: We agreed to ration. (*Ed leans back against the bench, crosses his arms, and sulks. Steve sits up and grumbles.*) Now I can't sleep.

ED: You'll get plenty of sleep real soon.

STEVE (*lethargic*): You make me sick. (*Ed pulls some cards out of his pocket and plays solitaire on the floor. Steve picks up two empty cans and begins stacking them and knocking them over. Wendy touches her wound. She cries quietly. Steve speaks harshly.*) There she goes again.

ED: Always making a racket.

Wendy's sobs increase in spite of her extreme effort to stop.

STEVE: Can't you be quiet? We're tired of hearing you all the time. We can't sleep, we can't think.

WENDY (*now crying uncontrollably*): My arm . . .

ED: We don't give a *damn* about your arm.

STEVE: You should have been more careful in the first place.

Janet goes over to her. Wendy pulls her arm away at first, then holds it out to her. Janet unwraps it, and Wendy slowly stops crying.

JANET: What have you been putting on it?

WENDY: That stuff that was in the first aid kit. It's all gone now.

JANET: This needs to be cleaned.

She goes toward the water barrel. Steve stands up and blocks her path.

STEVE: What are you doing?

JANET: She's badly infected.

STEVE: I don't care if her arm rots off, you're not using any of our water. (*Janet starts to walk around him. He grabs her by the arm. She struggles, and he slaps her face. Everyone freezes. Steve's grip slowly loosens from her arm.*) Janet, I . . . (*Janet goes to the water barrel and fills a cup. Steve's body goes limp as he sits.*) What's happening to us? Janet, I'm so sorry. I don't know how—

Janet returns to Wendy with the water, kneels, and cleans the wound.

ED (*to Janet*): That's coming out of your ration.

Janet works in silence, then—

JANET: Where are the bandages?

WENDY: This was the last one.

Janet thinks a moment before tearing a strip from the bottom of her own shirt.

JANET: Steve, give me a match.

He hands her one. Janet lights a candle and holds the cloth by its ends so that the middle of it is over the flame.

WENDY: What are you doing?

STEVE: Sterilizing it.

She moves to Wendy.

WENDY: Let it cool off some.

Janet waits a few seconds.

JANET: Here we go. (*She applies the bandage.*) That didn't hurt, did it?

Wendy shakes her head. Then her face twists in sorrow.

WENDY (*quietly, but with great emotion*): I wish it was all over. I can't stand it anymore. (*Janet pulls her close and strokes her hair as Wendy quietly speaks.*) I don't mean to cause so much trouble. Really I don't.

JANET: I know.

WENDY: It's just that I'm so scared. Why did they do it? Why did they have to go and do it?

JANET: I don't know.

WENDY: Everything was so good before.

JANET: Try and sleep. You'll feel better.

Wendy closes her eyes. Janet rocks her slowly from side to side.

ED: I'm through waiting. If you don't give me my ration, I'll take it myself. And don't tell me it's not time yet, because it is.

STEVE: I was just about to get it when you started your yapping.

Steve pulls a can of beans out of a crate.

ED: Hurry up. (*Steve opens the can, pours a small amount of beans into several tin plates and passes them along. He then fills several mugs with water.*) Janet already had hers. (*Steve gives a mug to everyone but Janet. Wendy shares with her. Ed looks at Steve's plate.*) Wait a minute! You have more food than anyone else!

STEVE: You always say that. If you don't like the way I dish out the rations, do it yourself.

ED: All right.

He reaches for Steve's plate. A scuffle ensues, and all the beans are spilled onto the floor.

WENDY: Stop!

Ed and Steve start picking up beans and putting them into their plates. Then they each move to a different part of the shelter to eat. Steve keeps casting furtive glances at Ed. Ed keeps glancing at all three of the others.

ED: I know what you're thinking. You're thinking about how low on food we're getting. You're thinking about who to eat first. Well, I'm keeping my eyes on you.

JANET: Ed, you're just being—

Janet turns and points her fork at Ed as she speaks. Ed, high with tension, cringes backward and holds up his own fork in a convulsive reflex action. When he realizes he is in no danger, he begins to pick up the beans that flew when he jumped.

ED: I think we should divide up the rest of the food now. Make each person responsible for their own.

STEVE: That's fine with me. Janet?

JANET: I don't care.

Steve passes out a few packets of dehydrated food and a couple of cans to each of them. Ed huddles possessively over his.

ED: What about the water?

STEVE: We don't have any extra containers. You'll just have to trust me.

ED (*angrily*): If you think—

A metallic banging causes everyone to freeze. They look at the hatch. The banging is repeated.

ADAM (*from offstage*): Anybody home?

WENDY: It's Adam!

ED: Don't let him in!

Janet moves to open the hatch. Ed steps in her way. She stares at him evenly.

JANET: Touch me, and I'll kill you in your sleep.

He steps aside. Janet opens the hatch. Adam is shabbier than in the first scene, but is still very lively. He carries his duffle bag down the ladder.

ADAM: Greetings. The prodigal son has returned.

ED: You're not getting any of my food.

ADAM: I wouldn't dream of it, Ed. We have to get you fattened up.

A strange man descends the ladder after Adam. His clothes are disheveled and torn, and his skin looks leprous, but his movements are quick and agile, like a spider.

WENDY: Who's that?

ADAM: This is Thomas, a friend I picked up on the outside.

THOMAS: He came to visit my shelter with his Message of Happy Doom. We were right at that stage where hunger circumvents morality. My companions took him a little too seriously when he suggested they eat me first. Adam and I had to exit hastily.

ADAM: That reminds me: Thomas, I'd like you to meet Ed. He's the first one they're going to eat in this shelter.

THOMAS: Of course. I've heard all about Ed.

Thomas eyes Ed up and down, smacking his lips.

ED: I'll kill you!

Ed slugs Adam in the eye, knocking him to the floor. Steve grabs Ed. Adam lies there, rubbing his eye. He smiles.

ADAM: Careful, Ed. It was that kind of thinking got us into this mess in the first place. Besides . . . (*He climbs up.*) . . . I come in peace. I bring gifts and good news. First, let me say how sorry I am that all of you missed our party. It was a grand affair.

STEVE: You actually had the party?

ADAM: Certainly. I don't mean to brag, but it will probably be known as the social event of the season.

WENDY: People really came?

ADAM: Absolutely. Quite interesting people, too.

THOMAS (*ironically*): Quite. Walking around in radiation tends to bring out the most unique character traits.

ADAM: Thomas here is a scientist.

THOMAS: One of the "guests of honor."

ADAM: All of the guests of honor were scientists. It's a funny thing, but we just couldn't get any generals to come to our party. We went to the military shelter and shouted down our invitation, but they refused to come out. Nothing could induce them, so we finally just left them to their thoughts and continued on our journey.

THOMAS: Maybe they wouldn't come because they didn't feel as guilty as we did. The generals didn't know what they were doing. We scientists should have known better. (*Pause*) I actually considered suicide for a while, until Adam showed me a better way to atone for my guilt.

ADAM: Which brings us to the matter of gifts mentioned earlier. I have here in my little bag of tricks: an air purifier. Handy gadget for these small shelters.

He pulls a small machine out of his bag.

JANET: Air purifier?

ADAM: Yes. Thomas made it himself. Tom, why don't you set it up, while I tell everyone about our travels. (*Thomas places the air purifier up against the bench. He gets down on one knee and begins making adjustments with a wrench. Adam declaims to the others—*) Gather around and I'll tell you of our adventures. After the party broke up, Thomas and I began a trek across the dead planet. It was a glorious sight. Miles and miles of shattered buildings, fitting monuments to the accomplishments of man. (*Ed rises.*) Don't go, Ed. You'll miss the good news.

ED: What good news?

ADAM: Just be patient. I'll come to it. . . . Now, where was I? . . . Ah, yes. Thomas and I travelled from shelter to shelter, spreading my Message of Happy Doom. Usually we were met with distrust and disgust, and more than once we were threatened with bodily injury. But every now and then we would gain a convert who would start out on a trek of their own. Anyway, one day Thomas and I were walking along, minding everybody's business, when he noticed a strange aroma. After a moment, I noticed it, too. It seemed to be coming from just over the next hill. When we reached the summit and looked over, we couldn't believe our eyes.

WENDY: What did you see?

ADAM: There was this long, thin valley, wedged in between two cliffs. It had obviously been formed by erosion.

ED: You saw a valley. Big deal.

ADAM: This valley was filled with plant life.

STEVE: Plant life!

ADAM: Yes. Thomas figures that with the way it's wedged in between those cliffs, it must have escaped the radiation that swept across. We went down to investigate, and Tom assures me that many of the plants are edible.

STEVE: Edible!

WENDY: That's great!

ADAM: Furthermore, they must be getting water from an uncontaminated, underwater spring.

WENDY: We're saved!

STEVE: I knew something had to happen. I just knew it. There had to be some reason why we were saved from the blast.

ED: What are we waiting for? Let's go!

ADAM: It's a really long way, and Tom and I are tired. I think it would be better if we start out fresh in the morning.

STEVE: That's a good idea. We'll start first thing tomorrow. Let's pack anything we want to keep. I don't want to have to come back here.

Steve, Ed, and Wendy start filling duffle bags with items from the crates. Janet and Adam sit on a pair of crates. They lean back against the wall.

WENDY: I just can't believe it. Plants and water.

Thomas turns a crank and the machine begins working. It makes a light pocketa-pocketa noise. Thomas leans up to a nozzle which is sticking out of the top of the machine, takes a deep breath, and slumps to the floor in back of the bench. No one has noticed him. They continue to talk excitedly.

STEVE: This is a big responsibility we have now. We've been given a second chance. It's up to us to rebuild the world. We've got to make sure we don't repeat the same mistakes that were made the first time. Out of the rubble of the dead world, we'll build a better one.

WENDY: Are we going to bring anyone from any of the other shelters?

STEVE: We'll have to. We can't repopulate by ourselves.

ED: We will have to do that . . . repopulate . . . won't we? (*He casts a quick glance at Wendy.*) I mean, it's sort of a duty, isn't it?

STEVE: Yes. We have to replenish the earth.

Steve sits on the edge of the bench. Yawns.

WENDY: Will we still have marriages and all like that?

STEVE: We'll have to have some kind of laws. We can decide all that when we get everyone to the valley. (*yawns*) I'm getting kind of sleepy. (*Wendy and Ed also show signs of sleepiness, such as blinking and yawning. Steve continues to talk, his speech growing more slurred and incoherent as he goes.*) I just can't believe our good fortune.

It's like a second Garden of Eden. And we were chosen. It will be from our loins that the new race will spring. (*Ed sits down and closes his eyes. Wendy does likewise.*) Hundreds of years from now, they'll write histories about us. About the valley. About how, about how the world was reborn. (*He slides to the floor.*) Reborn. Like a phoenix, out of its ashes. They'll make legends. They'll tell about how . . . about how . . .

He slumps over. The only sound is the pocketa-pocketa of the machine. Janet turns to Adam.

JANET: There is no valley, is there?

ADAM: No.

(*Pause*)

JANET: Thank you.

She closes her eyes. He watches her seriously for a moment, then closes his own eyes. The lights dim as the only sound is that of the machine. It chokes, sputters, then dies in a whimper.

Curtain

SPECIMENS UNDER GLASS

A Play in Three Acts

ACT ONE

Scene One

Scene is the large living room of an old, dilapidated apartment in New York City. The room is cluttered with filing cabinets, chairs, a desk, a couch, and numerous bookcases. Books are stacked everywhere: on the desk, on the furniture, even on the floor. In the corner is a kitchenette with a sink and short counter dividing it from the living room. In the center of the Upstage wall is a door leading outside. This door is flanked by a closet on one side and a desk with several chairs on the other. An open door in the Stage Right wall leads to the bedrooms. Beside this is a small wall mirror.

As the scene opens, a shabby looking character is lying flat on the floor beside the couch, parallel to the front of the stage. He is completely still, and at first glance might almost appear dead. Down on one knee beside the body is Sebastian Dumas (doo-MAH). He is writing in a notebook. After a few seconds, he takes a small, doctor's hammer out of his shirt pocket and taps the man's knee. Nothing happens. Sebastian records the results in his notebook. Then he takes the man's pulse and writes in the notebook once again. To get another perspective on the body, he stands and slowly backs up to the desk at Up Left, scrutinizing the body all the time. He rubs his chin as he leans against the desk and contemplates the body. There is a knock at the door.

SEBASTIAN: Nobody's home! (*He continues to look at the body. The knock is repeated, louder than before.*) Don't you believe me? (*Once again we hear the inevitable rapping sound, louder still.*) All right, come in!

Enter Mrs. Vail, the landlady, a dried up old woman.

VAIL: Mr. Dumas, if you think it's funny to leave me standing out there like— (*She stops dead when she sees the body.*) Who's that?

SEBASTIAN (*nonchalant, still looking at the body*): I don't know.

VAIL: What do you mean you don't know? He's lying in the middle of your floor!

SEBASTIAN: Nevertheless, I have no idea who he is.

VAIL: You mean you just came into your apartment and found him here?

SEBASTIAN: No. I found him in Central Park. If nobody claims him in sixty days, I get to keep him. (*Mrs. Vail looks at him as if she thinks he's crazy.*) What's wrong? Don't you think he'd make a unique conversation piece?

VAIL: I think he'd probably make good grounds for a criminal investigation.

SEBASTIAN: Come on, you know I wouldn't keep anything that didn't belong to me. If they can find the rightful owner, I'll gladly give him back.

VAIL: Look, Mr. Dumas, there are a lot of nice apartments in New York. Why don't you find some other place to live?

SEBASTIAN: I like it here. Besides, Lance and I have another six months to go on our lease.

VAIL: Leases can be broken.

SEBASTIAN: Not by me.

VAIL: You could be forced to leave.

SEBASTIAN: I'm afraid you'd find me a difficult tenant to evict, Mrs. Vail. Bigger men than you have tried.

VAIL: Well, I didn't come up here to argue. I came because the first of the month was two weeks ago, and you still haven't—

SEBASTIAN (*dismissing her with a wave of his hand*): Whatever it is will have to wait, Mrs. Vail. I'm extremely busy right now and don't have time to stand around chatting, so if you will excuse me . . .

He moves to the body and kneels down. Mrs. Vail watches as he pulls back one of the man's eyelids and lets it snap back. He starts to write in his notebook.

VAIL: Mr. Dumas—

SEBASTIAN: Shhhh.

VAIL: I really must insist that you—

SEBASTIAN (*forcefully*): Quiet.

VAIL: Really, Mr. Dumas, if you're going to continue—

SEBASTIAN (*exasperated*): Mrs. Vail, must you always interrupt me while I'm working?

VAIL: I don't think I approve of your work, Mr. Dumas, whatever it is, and I don't think I want you doing it in the apartment anymore. Furthermore, if you don't give me the—

SEBASTIAN: Mrs. Vail, you don't realize what you're saying. I'm making some very important discoveries here. Someday when I publish my findings, this broken down old apartment you run will be famous.

VAIL: I don't want to be famous. I just want you to pay me the money you owe me.

SEBASTIAN: Ah, so now we come to it. (*He rises.*) The moment you walked through the door, I knew you had some ulterior motive. Why is it you never pay us a social call, Mrs. Vail? Every time you come up here, you're begging for handouts. Don't you have any pride?

VAIL: I'm not begging for handouts. I'm collecting the rent.

SEBASTIAN: Well, if you want to argue semantics . . .

VAIL: I don't want to argue semantics. I want you to pay your rent.

SEBASTIAN: Look, if you're really hard up, I suppose I could spare a little something. (*He pulls some coins out of his pocket and counts them in his palm.*) Would a dollar seventy-three help? (*She glares at him.*) If that's not enough, I suppose I could dig around in the sofa cushions.

VAIL: This is ridiculous! Every month I come up here, and every month we go through some silly rigmarole. Why don't you just pay like everyone else?

SEBASTIAN: If everyone else is paying, why do you have to come begging around here?

VAIL: Mr. Dumas!

SEBASTIAN: All right, calm down. Lance will be home any minute. You can get the money from him.

VAIL: I think it's shameful the way you take advantage

of poor Mr. Montgomery. He's had to pay the rent every month now. I'll bet you don't even pay him back, do you?

SEBASTIAN: What do you care where the money comes from? After all, beggars can't be choosers.

VAIL: I told you, I'm not begging.

SEBASTIAN: Semantics, Mrs. Vail.

VAIL: Well, I can't wait around here all afternoon. I have some errands to run, but I'd better get my money when I come back.

She exits.

SEBASTIAN (*to himself*): Noisy old panhandler. (*He kneels down beside the body and continues his examination. Then we hear a noise like someone kicking the door.*) Come in!

LANCE (*from offstage*): It's me—Lance! I've got groceries!

SEBASTIAN: Okay, bring 'em on in!

There is a brief pause, then the door opens to reveal Lance Montgomery, a frail, anemic individual who, up until six months ago, had the innocence and trust of a puppy dog, but is rapidly learning the ways of the world at the hands of Sebastian. His natural innocence is still his strongest feature, however, causing him to be the perennial dupe.
He now enters the apartment carrying two oversize sacks of

groceries, and from the way he's struggling, we realize he's liable to get a hernia. He wobbles over to the table in back of the couch, sets down the sacks, and stands there, gasping for air. He looks at Sebastian and the body.

LANCE: I wish you wouldn't bring your specimens into the house.

SEBASTIAN: Isn't he a beauty? He's one of the finest I've ever had in my collection.

LANCE: He looks dead.

SEBASTIAN (*proudly*): Doesn't he, though? I think he may well be the laziest human alive. He's been lying in Central Park for weeks, and the only muscles he's ever moved are his jaw muscles when he chews. He's practically famous. Old men who have been coming to the park for years to feed the pigeons have started feeding him instead.

LANCE: Couldn't you have left him in the park? I'm getting a little tired of having your specimens around here all the time.

SEBASTIAN: You know that if I'm going to make a systematic study of the human race, I have to have my specimens close at hand where I can observe them carefully.

LANCE: I just don't understand why you have to study

the whole human race one at a time.

SEBASTIAN: I don't. But I do have to study each *type* individually. Each of my specimens represents a condensation of some particular human trait. This week I'm studying lethargy. If I were a botanist, you wouldn't fault me for bringing plant specimens home. As a philosopher, I have to study human specimens.

LANCE (*uncertainly*): I guess so.

SEBASTIAN: Certainly. Now why don't you put away the groceries while I finish up these notes?

LANCE: Okay.

Lance carries one of the sacks to the kitchen area and begins putting away the groceries as Sebastian moves to the chair at Down Left and starts writing in his notebook.

SEBASTIAN: Oh, Lance, what time do you have?

LANCE (*checking his watch*): Almost two.

SEBASTIAN: Would you mind feeding my specimen for me? I want to get this finished.

LANCE: Okay. (*He crosses to the body.*) What should I feed him?

SEBASTIAN: Anything. He won't complain.

Lance looks through the sack which is still on the table and comes up with a banana. He kneels beside the body and peels the banana, then stops as he realizes he has no idea how to proceed.

LANCE: Um, Sebastian . . .

SEBASTIAN: Yeah?

LANCE: What do I do?

SEBASTIAN: Hold the food under his nose. When he smells it, his mouth will open.

Lance breaks off a piece of banana and feeds it to the specimen.

LANCE: Hey, it works.

SEBASTIAN: Sure.

Lance breaks off another piece and goes through the procedure again.

LANCE: How long are we going to keep this one?

SEBASTIAN: Just a few days. So don't grow attached to him.

LANCE: I won't. (*He feeds him another piece.*) How come you've got to study him a few days? I mean, if he never says anything and never moves, it doesn't seem there'd be much you could find out.

SEBASTIAN: I have a few tests I want to run. For one thing, I want to see if I can get him to respond to any stimuli other than food.

LANCE (*feeding him another piece of banana*): He seems to like *that* well enough.

SEBASTIAN: Yes, he does.

Lance feeds the last of the banana to the specimen, then looks up at Sebastian, who has been writing furiously this whole time.

LANCE: You sure are writing a lot of notes on this guy.

SEBASTIAN: Not really. Most of what I'm writing now has to do with a field experiment I conducted this morning. I want to get it all down while the details are still fresh in my mind.

LANCE (*nervously*): You conducted a field experiment this morning?

SEBASTIAN: That's right.

Lance rises and comes over to Sebastian.

LANCE (*uncertainly*): Hey, Sebastian . . . this isn't one of those field experiments where the police are going to come around asking a bunch of questions again, is it?

SEBASTIAN: Possibly.

LANCE: I knew it! Why do you keep doing these things? You know Mrs. Vail said if the police have to come up here one more time, she's going to toss us into the street.

SEBASTIAN: I doubt that. Mrs. Vail is a very small woman.

LANCE: I'm serious, Sebastian. You've got to stop pulling these practical jokes.

SEBASTIAN: I told you before, they're not practical jokes. They're carefully constructed experiments designed to gauge human responses to unusual stimuli.

LANCE: To you, they're experiments, but to the people you do them to, they're practical jokes.

SEBASTIAN: What other choice do I have? I'm not like a scientist, who can perform his experiments in a laboratory. I'm a philosopher. The world is my laboratory. People are my guinea pigs.

LANCE: But people don't want to be your guinea pigs. It's tough enough being people. Really, Sebastian, you're making me very tense.

SEBASTIAN: Why are *you* tense?

LANCE: Because last time you went on a field experiment you used *my* name.

SEBASTIAN: So?

LANCE: So I went to jail!

SEBASTIAN: Only for one night.

LANCE: It was terrible!

SEBASTIAN: That's just because you didn't know how to take advantage of your situation. If you were a philosopher, you'd have used your time productively. Take Thoreau, for instance. He spent *his* night in jail contemplating great universal truths.

LANCE: I spent *my* night in jail trying to keep an old wino from using me as a toilet.

SEBASTIAN: Maybe they'll put you in a better cell this time.

LANCE: Why would they put me in a cell? What did you do?

SEBASTIAN: Are you sure you want to know?

LANCE: Yes, I want to know. Last time I didn't know anything was wrong until they read me my rights.

SEBASTIAN: Okay. As you know, lately I've been studying the human phenomenon of blind obedience to authority. I began by examining the way people react to their bosses and the way children react to their parents, but the more I studied it, the more I realized that people will blindly follow *anyone* who approaches them as an authority figure. Then it struck me. Suppose I were to dress up in a suit and tie, go into some place of business, and tell them I was there in an official capacity? How far could I carry it before someone figured out it was a hoax? I decided to perform a field experiment to find out, so I donned the superficial garments of authority, picked up a clipboard and a pen, and went down to *Aiello's*. You know, the Italian place with the great lasagna?

LANCE: Yeah.

SEBASTIAN: I went in and told them I was the State Health Inspector.

LANCE: That's impersonating a government official!

SEBASTIAN: If you want to be technical. Anyway, I then proceeded to inspect the place. I examined everything: the food, the equipment. And the amazing thing was, nobody asked to see my credentials. The suit was enough. I've been in *Aiello's*—what, a hundred times?—and I've never even gotten good service, but I go in there with a suit, a clipboard, and a title, and they roll out the red carpet. Old Mr. Aiello even made me a House Special with his own two hands. You should have seen the look on his face when I suddenly clutched my stomach, fell to the floor, and started yelling, "ptomaine, ptomaine!"

LANCE: You didn't!

SEBASTIAN: I did. They were ready to call the hospital, but I began to recover after someone brought me a seltzer.

LANCE: Did they ever find out you were a phony?

SEBASTIAN: Not a chance. I played my part to perfection.

LANCE: Thank goodness for that. So it's all over?

SEBASTIAN: Sort of.

LANCE: What do you mean, sort of?

SEBASTIAN: I closed them down.

LANCE (*aghast*): How could you do that?

SEBASTIAN: I put a sign on the door that said, "Closed by Order of the State Health Inspector."

LANCE: But you're not the State Health Inspector!

SEBASTIAN: You've got to admit, *Aiello's* has never been very sanitary.

LANCE: That's beside the point! People can't just go around closing down restaurants they don't like.

SEBASTIAN: *I* did.

LANCE: Please, Sebastian, if you don't stop pulling these . . . experiments of yours, one of us is going to end up in prison.

SEBASTIAN: Don't worry. I didn't use your name this time.

LANCE: Did you use your own?

SEBASTIAN: I'm not that foolish. Look, don't worry about it. All that's going to happen is, Mr. Aiello is going to clean up his place a little, I'll go back in a few days for another inspection . . .

LANCE: You're going back?

SEBASTIAN: Certainly. I have to give Aiello permission to reopen.

LANCE (*holds his head and sits down*): I don't think I can take it anymore.

Sebastian goes up to him and puts his hand on his shoulder.

SEBASTIAN: Actually, I'm performing an important service, Lance. If you don't shake people up every now and then, they tend to stagnate. That's why I always have to—

He is interrupted by a knock at the door. Lance's head pops up.

LANCE: The police!

SEBASTIAN: That's impossible. (*He goes to the door and looks out the peephole.*) Oh, it's just that old woman who was here earlier begging for alms. I tried to get rid of her, but you know how desperate these bag women can be. You talk to her. I'll be back in my bedroom.

LANCE: Wait, Sebastian, what . . . ? (*Sebastian exits. Lance goes to the door and opens it to reveal Mrs. Vail.*) Oh, Mrs. Vail, it's you.

VAIL: Yes, I was up here earlier. I assume your roommate told you.

LANCE: Sort of.

VAIL: I'm here to collect the rent, and I won't be put off. If you don't pay me today, I'll have to start eviction proceedings.

LANCE: I have the money right here. I was paid today and went straight to the bank to cash my check.

He pulls some money out of his pocket and begins to count it.

VAIL: I'll write you a receipt. (*She starts to dig in her purse.*) I know it's none of my business, and I'm the last one who'd butt into anyone's affairs, but why don't you ever make Mr. Dumas pay his share of the rent?

LANCE: Well, he's out of work right now.

VAIL: I thought his work had something to do with . . .

She indicates the body.

LANCE: No, that's different. He doesn't get paid for that.

VAIL: Well, is he trying to find a job?

LANCE: I don't know, really. I've brought it up a few times, but I've never quite understood his answer.

VAIL: You'd better bring it up again. If you're late with the rent one more time, I'm going to have to have you evicted.

LANCE: Yes, ma'am.

VAIL (*closing her purse*): I seem to have left my receipt book downstairs. Have you counted out the money?

LANCE: Here it is.

He hands it over.

VAIL: All right. I'll go back down to my place and write you a receipt.

LANCE: Thank you.

He opens the door for her.

VAIL: Remember what I said.

LANCE: Yes, ma'am.

Vail exits. Lance stands there, thinking. Sebastian enters.

SEBASTIAN: Is she gone?

LANCE: Yes.

SEBASTIAN: Good. I hate watching people beg.

He goes back to his chair and picks up a book. Lance approaches him uncertainly.

LANCE: Sebastian, I think we need to have a talk.

SEBASTIAN: Okay.

LANCE: A serious talk.

Sebastian sets down his book and looks at Lance.

SEBASTIAN: All right.

LANCE: First off, I want you to know that I realize your studies take up a lot of your time, and I never would have brought this up if it weren't getting so hard to make ends meet around here . . .

SEBASTIAN: We'd be doing all right if you'd go ahead and get that second job like I suggested.

LANCE: But that's just it. I don't want a second job. That's why we need to have this talk. Do you realize that you've been living here for six months now and you still haven't found work?

SEBASTIAN: What do you mean "still?"

LANCE: I mean that in the whole time I've known you, you've never had a job.

SEBASTIAN: That's not surprising, considering I haven't been looking for one.

LANCE: You haven't?

SEBASTIAN: No.

LANCE: Why not?

SEBASTIAN: I don't have to work. I'm a philosopher.

LANCE: Are philosophers *always* unemployed?

SEBASTIAN: It's practically mandatory.

LANCE: How do they earn a living?

SEBASTIAN: They don't. A true philosopher spends his time conducting his studies and leaves the money grubbing to others.

LANCE: But they have to eat.

SEBASTIAN: In order to take care of the physical necessities like food and shelter, a philosopher must find a patron, someone to take over the chores of making money and provide him a haven where he can meditate in safety.

LANCE: Is that what I am?

SEBASTIAN: That's right. You're my patron.

LANCE: I don't want to be a patron.

SEBASTIAN: That's not for you to decide. Each of us has to do what we're most qualified for. I have the education and training of a philosopher, you have the intelligence and temperament of a patron. Actually, yours is a very noble profession, Lance. You're helping to keep a great philosopher alive. Someday your name will go down in history alongside those of Aristotle's mentor, Socrates' wife, and Galileo's caterer.

LANCE: Couldn't my name just sort of stand off by itself somewhere?

SEBASTIAN: And what would you have *me* do? Abandon my studies and get a job? If I'm going to advance the state of philosophy, I must remain unfettered. The human spirit must be allowed to soar.

LANCE: I'd like my spirit to soar, too.

SEBASTIAN: Listen, Lance, there are two kinds of people in the world: those whose spirits soar, and the drones. Unfortunate, perhaps, but such is the way of things. I happen to be a philosopher, one of those whose spirits soar; and you, alas, happen to be a drone. Now, if that explains matters, I have some reading to do.

He picks up his book.

LANCE: Wait a minute. That doesn't explain matters. You still expect me to pay your share of the rent and food. When I put an ad in the newspaper asking for someone to share an apartment, I meant I wanted them to share the rent and expenses, not just share the apartment.

SEBASTIAN: I'll tell you what, Lance. I can see you're dissatisfied with your lot in life, so I'm going to do something for you that I've never done for anyone before.

LANCE: You'll get a job?

SEBASTIAN: No. I'm going to teach you to be a philosopher.

LANCE: That's not what I—

SEBASTIAN: Oh, I grant you it'll be hard work at first. But just think of the benefits. As a philosopher, you'll be master of your own destiny. You and I will walk side by side through a world of fools and knaves, secure in the knowledge that we're controllers of Fate.

LANCE: I think I'd rather just—

SEBASTIAN: Come over here, Lance. (*He goes to the bookcase. Lance follows.*) I'm going to start you out with a good, comprehensive history of philosophy. That way you'll get a broad overview of the different schools of thought. (*He pulls down a volume which resembles an unabridged dictionary in size and mass and hands it to Lance.*) There you go.

LANCE (*faltering under its weight*): I have to read this?

SEBASTIAN: Yes.

LANCE: Couldn't you just tell me what it's about?

SEBASTIAN: You have to make some sacrifices if you want to be a philosopher.

LANCE (*agitated*): I never said I wanted to—

SEBASTIAN: Perhaps you're right. (*He takes the book from him.*) This *is* a bit much for a beginner. I think I have something that would suit you better. (*He searches the shelf.*) Ah, here it is.

He pulls out a much smaller, paperbound volume and hands it to Lance.

LANCE (*reading the title*): "Philosophy—Duh"?

SEBASTIAN: It's a condensation of philosophical thought for the general public. After you've gone through that and decided which philosophers you like, I'll give you some more specialized reading. But that's just the first step. Once you've gotten a good theoretical foundation, I'll start taking you in the field with me, letting you try out the things you've learned. Then it won't be long before you start collecting specimens of your own and conducting your own experiments.

LANCE: How long before I can get my own patron?

SEBASTIAN: I'll let you know when you're ready. But first, you have to start reading.

LANCE (*opening the book reluctantly*): Where should I start?

SEBASTIAN: Anywhere.

Lance thumbs through the book, then stops. He mumbles—

LANCE: *The Will to Power* by Friedrich Nee . . . Nich . . .

SEBASTIAN: Nietzsche.

LANCE: Nietzsche.

SEBASTIAN: Are you sure you want to start with him?

LANCE (*to himself*): *The Will to Power . . .* (*to Sebastian*) Yes. This is the one.

SEBASTIAN (*chuckles*): Okay. Let me know if you have any trouble. I'll be back in my bedroom changing clothes.

LANCE: Are you going out again?

SEBASTIAN: Yes, they're having a big political rally in Washington Square. I'm hoping to pick up a few new specimens.

Sebastian exits. Lance reads as he puts away the last of the groceries. Several times he bumps into the counter or drops things on the floor because he is so busy concentrating on the book. Then he stops.

LANCE (*calling out*): Hey, Sebastian!

SEBASTIAN (*sticking his head through the door*): Yeah?

LANCE: This is a little hard to understand, but it seems like what he's teaching is Survival of the Most Violent.

SEBASTIAN (*laughs*): You're on the right track. Just hold

that idea.

LANCE: Okay. (*Sebastian disappears. Lance contemplates—*) Survival of the Most Violent. (*He growls.*) Rrrr! (*He goes and looks at himself in the mirror.*) Grrr! Arggh! Growr! Aaargh!!

The door opens and Mrs. Vail enters.

VAIL: Here's your . . .

LANCE (*whirls on her*): Aaarrghhh!!

VAIL (*jumping back and running out the door*) Oooohhh!!

Lance looks at the philosophy book with new respect.

LANCE: Hey, this philosophy stuff really works. (*He looks in the mirror.*) Rrrr!

SEBASTIAN (*entering*): Say, Lance . . .

LANCE: Aaarghh!!

SEBASTIAN (*jumping back*): What are you doing?

LANCE (*meekly*): Being a Nietzscheist.

SEBASTIAN (*scolding*): Well, stop it.

LANCE: You told me I could be a philosopher.

SEBASTIAN: Not a Nietzscheist. Find something else.

Lance sits down and thumbs through the book.

LANCE (*pouting*): I wanted to be a Nietzscheist. (*to Sebastian*) How about Aristotle?

SEBASTIAN: He's good. Now you sit there and read. I'll be back later.

Sebastian exits. Lance reads.

LANCE: "Some men are born to be slaves, others are born to be masters." (*He looks at the door where Sebastian has just exited.*) That's the truth. (*He reads again, then stops and muses.*) Some men are born to be slaves, others are born to be masters. (*He slams the book closed.*) Well, I'm through being one of the slaves. From now on, I'm going to be one of the masters!

He rises and quickly exits.

Blackout

ACT ONE

Scene Two

Same scene as before, later that day. Sebastian enters with three members of the Radical Homeless Youth Brigade—Tomás, Edgar, and Mitya. They are all dressed in black leather jackets and berets, and each of them has a minimum of three weapons hanging from their belts. (Chains, knives, etc.) As they enter, Sebastian and Tomás are arguing.

TOMÁS: No, I'm saying we've moved beyond the era of rational thought. We must now embrace the era of brute force.

SEBASTIAN: Then how will you keep the industries running? It takes more that brute force to run a generator.

TOMÁS: It takes more than brute force to *build* a generator. But the generators are all built and in place.

SEBASTIAN: So you're saying you can't *build* the world, but you can *run* it without the men of intelligence?

EDGAR (*abrupt, vehement*): We'll kill them!

Everyone is startled and jumps slightly at this outburst.

SEBASTIAN (*startled*): What?

EDGAR (*almost shouting*): All intellectuals will hang from

the highest tree!

SEBASTIAN (*bemused*): Isn't that a bit drastic?

EDGAR: No! All intellectuals will be shot! They will be hung! They will be boiled in oil!

TOMÁS: What Edgar is trying to say is: intellectualism is a cancer which eats away at the moral base of a revolution.

Sebastian looks from Tomás to Edgar, then back to Tomás.

SEBASTIAN: Are you *sure* that's what he's trying to say?

TOMÁS: Yes. Overly cerebral people would kill the revolution.

SEBASTIAN (*smiling*): I think: therefore I'm not a good revolutionary.

TOMÁS: Don't twist my words. We *do* want people to think. It's just that we want them to think with their gut.

EDGAR: People who think with their brains will be mashed under giant stones! They will be crushed beneath large, teeming—

TOMÁS: I think he gets the picture.

SEBASTIAN: No one could accuse Edgar of being overly

cerebral.

EDGAR (*brightly*): Thank you.

SEBASTIAN: But where are my manners? Come in and sit down, everyone. Let me get you something to drink.

He heads for the kitchen area as Edgar and Mitya move to the couch.

TOMÁS (*going with Sebastian*): I'll help you.

Edgar and Mitya stare at the body they had to step over on their way to the couch.

EDGAR: Is this guy dead?

SEBASTIAN: No. Just noncommittal.

EDGAR (*quietly, automatically*): All noncommittal people will have their eyes plucked out.

TOMÁS: Is that the roommate you were telling us about?

SEBASTIAN: No. He's just visiting.

MITYA (*looking around*): We've got twelve people living in a place this size. How many people you got living here?

SEBASTIAN: Two.

MITYA: Two?

EDGAR: It's decadent.

SEBASTIAN: Yes, but we call it home. (*Sebastian and Tomás join the others and hand them their drinks.*) Here you go. (*Tomás settles into one of the chairs.*) So, tell me more about this "Dollars for Bullets" campaign you're running. It sounds fascinating.

TOMÁS: What we're trying to do is, instead of running this revolution from the top, down, or from the bottom, up, we're trying to run it from the middle, out. Our "Dollars for Bullets" campaign is designed to get middle class Americans to help finance a military occupation of New York State as a beginning to a homeless revolution on the east coast.

SEBASTIAN: How much money have you raised.

TOMÁS: None. But the success of any fund raising campaign is measured by the amount that it raises social consciousness, not by the actual amount of money raised.

EDGAR (*confused as a sudden thought occurs to him*): But if it's a fund raising campaign, and we don't raise any funds . . .

TOMÁS (*testily*): You can't measure the success of any campaign by its actual results.

EDGAR (*still confused*): But . . .

At this moment the door slams open and Lance stumbles through. His clothes are disheveled and torn, his face is scratched; he looks as if he's just been through a blender.

SEBASTIAN: What happened to you?

LANCE (*leaning back against the door jamb with his arms pressed against it for support*): Oh, it was terrible. It was terrible.

SEBASTIAN: Here, let me help you. (*He helps him toward the couch.*) Can you make it? You want some water?

Lance nods.

TOMÁS: I'll get it.

He goes to the kitchen area.

SEBASTIAN: Are you hurt?

LANCE (*rambling*): I'll never do anything like that again. Never.

Tomás steps up with the water.

TOMÁS: Here.

SEBASTIAN: Drink this. (*Lance drinks.*) Can you tell us

about it?

LANCE: You remember when you told me to read Aristotle?

SEBASTIAN: Yes. (*Lance vehemently shakes his head, indicating it was the worst decision of his life.*) What happened?

LANCE: I read the part where he said that some men are born to be slaves and others are born to be masters.

SEBASTIAN: So?

LANCE: So I went out looking for some slaves.

SEBASTIAN (*amused, proud of him*): You didn't.

LANCE: Why not? You've got a slave. I thought it was only fair I should have one.

SEBASTIAN: So what happened?

LANCE: Well, I was over on 42nd Street when I saw this group of guys who were obviously among those born to be slaves, so I went up to them and suggested they be mine.

SEBASTIAN: I take it they behaved in a most un-Aristotelian manner?

LANCE (*nodding*): They were downright Nietzscheists.

SEBASTIAN: Let me get you some more water.

He takes the glass.

LANCE: I think I'll go back to being a patron. This philosophy stuff is dangerous.

SEBASTIAN: Nonsense. You have to expect a few setbacks at first. The important thing is, you jumped right in there and gave it a shot. We'll make a philosopher out of you yet.

MITYA (*rushes over and sits in Lance's lap*): You poor baby. I'll make it better.

She started kissing him all over the face.

LANCE (*struggling*): Ouch! What's that?

Mitya looks down and sees that one of her weapons has been jabbing him in the side.

MITYA: Oh, that's my knife.

She slides it out of the way.

LANCE: Your knife!?

His struggles increase. She starts kissing him again. Edgar jumps up angrily.

EDGAR: Stop making love to my Mitya!

LANCE (*earnestly*): I'm not making love to your Mitya.

EDGAR (*pulls gun and aims it at him*): I said stop it!

LANCE (*in panic*): A Nietzscheist!

Sebastian jumps up and grabs Edgar's gun arm and aims it up.

SEBASTIAN: Whoa. Let's not get carried away here.

TOMÁS: Edgar, put that away.

EDGAR: But he's making love to my Mitya.

LANCE (*insistently*): I'm not making love to your Mitya.

TOMÁS: Mitya, get up from there. We're going now.

MITYA: Aw, come on, Tomás. Can't we stay just a few more minutes?

TOMÁS: No.

Mitya rises reluctantly, rubs her fingers under Lance's chin.

MITYA: I have to go now, but I'll be back, my little frail one.

TOMÁS: Come on. Let's go. (*to Sebastian*) You should come down to our headquarters sometime. It's only about a block from here.

SEBASTIAN: I'll do that.

The RHYB begin to exit.

MITYA (*to Lance*): You can count on it.

They leave. Sebastian goes back over to Lance.

SEBASTIAN (*proudly*): This has been quite a day for you. You had your first lesson in philosophy and got yourself a new girlfriend.

LANCE: I think she's dangerous. I think they're all dangerous.

SEBASTIAN: She obviously likes you.

LANCE: Yeah, but I don't think I'd want to go out with a girl who carries a knife. (*He thinks for a second.*) And I'm *sure* I wouldn't want to go out with a girl who has a boyfriend who carries a gun. (*There is a knock at the door. Lance, emphatically—*) Don't let them back in!

Sebastian goes to the door and looks out the peephole.

SEBASTIAN: It's just my sister.

LANCE: Oh, okay.

Sebastian opens the door. Lisa Dumas enters.

LISA: Hi, Bass.

SEBASTIAN: Hi, Lisa. (*They hug.*) You just get off work?

LISA: Yes. I had to be in the city tonight, so I thought I'd come by and— (*She suddenly notices Lance's condition.*) Lance! What happened to you?

SEBASTIAN: He stepped between a couple of conflicting ideas.

LISA: Here, let me look at it. (*She goes over and sits on the arm of the chair and examines the abrasions on Lance's face.*) Do you have any alcohol, Bass?

SEBASTIAN: I think there's some in the bathroom. Just a minute.

He exits.

LISA: Let me see the back of your head.

Lance turns his face away from her and she examines his skull, gently rubbing it with her fingertips. He winces several times.

LANCE: Am I bleeding?

LISA: No. You're pretty messed up, though. Want to tell me about it?

LANCE: It's a little hard to explain. You see, Sebastian was teaching me to be a philosopher, and things sort of got out of hand.

LISA: You didn't try to pull a field experiment, did you?

LANCE: No, I'm not advanced enough for that. I just tried to get me some slaves.

SEBASTIAN (*returning*): Here's the alcohol.

Lisa takes a handkerchief out of her purse.

LISA: What's this about you sending Lance out to get some slaves?

SEBASTIAN: All *I* did was set him to reading Aristotle. The slaves were his own idea.

LANCE (*in all fairness*): The slaves were Aristotle's idea. (*Lisa puts some alcohol on the handkerchief and starts to clean his wounds.)* Ouch!

LISA: Hold still.

LANCE: It burns.

LISA: It's supposed to burn. That helps you remember

not to do that again.

Sebastian picks up the philosophy book he had given Lance earlier and begins to look through it.

SEBASTIAN: Maybe you should try Spinoza next.

LANCE: Who's he?

SEBASTIAN: He's the philosopher who said that human suffering is trivial when considered in the context of eternity.

LANCE: Don't you have any philosophers who don't *want* me to suffer?

SEBASTIAN (*turning to another spot in the book*): Well, you could try—

LISA: I think Lance's had enough philosophy for one day. (*She grins at Sebastian.*) He hasn't built up a tolerance yet.

SEBASTIAN (*smiling*): Okay.

He puts the book down.

LISA: But that reminds me. (*She opens her purse.*) I have something for you.

She pulls out a book and hands it to Sebastian.

SEBASTIAN (*excited*): All right!

LANCE: What is it?

SEBASTIAN: It's that Saki collection I've been waiting for.

LISA: I thought you would be pleased.

SEBASTIAN (*thumbing through the volume*): "The Schartz-Metterklume Method" . . . "The Unrest Cure" . . . This is great. (*to Lance*) You should look through this sometime, Lance. A Saki collection reads like a case history of human experiments. (*Looks into the volume once again.*) He must have studied some interesting specimens in his time.

LISA (*indicates body*): I notice *you* have a new specimen.

SEBASTIAN: Yes, I got him just this morning. Would you like to examine him?

LISA (*laughs*): Maybe later.

SEBASTIAN: He has some very unique qualities.

LISA: I'm sure he does, but I really need to be going.

SEBASTIAN: So soon?

LISA: Yes. I've got a lot of shopping to do tonight. I had

planned to do it tomorrow, but it turns out I have to work all weekend.

SEBASTIAN: That's a shame.

LISA: I'll stop by on my way home, though.

SEBASTIAN: Okay.

She goes to the door.

LISA (*to Lance*): You take care of yourself.

LANCE: I will.

LISA (*to Sebastian*): Goodbye.

SEBASTIAN: Bye. (*She exits. Sebastian goes back over to Lance.*) How do you feel?

LANCE: I'm all right. Just a little sore.

SEBASTIAN: Would you like me to make you some soup or something?

LANCE: I'm not very hungry.

SEBASTIAN: Okay. Let me know if I can do anything for you. (*He goes to the couch, sits, and opens his Saki collection.*) Oh, I almost forgot. A letter came for you.

LANCE (*bewildered*): That's funny. I was here when the mail came, and all I noticed were a couple of bills.

SEBASTIAN: I don't mean it came today. This was last week sometime.

LANCE (*impatiently*): Well, where is it?

SEBASTIAN (*concentrating*): Let me see . . . (*He snaps his fingers.*) That's right. It's in the refrigerator.

LANCE (*rising angrily and going to the kitchen area*): What's it doing in there?

SEBASTIAN: I had to funnel some milk.

Lance opens the refrigerator and finds the envelope, wet and in the shape of a funnel.

LANCE (*disgusted*): It's all wet.

He straightens it out of the counter and blots it dry with a paper towel.

SEBASTIAN: Who's it from?

LANCE (*squinting at the envelope*): I can't read the return address. All the letters have blurred together. (*He opens it and begins to read the letter. Then, surprised, he says—*) It's from my Uncle Thaddeus. It says he's coming to New York for a few days and plans to stay with us.

SEBASTIAN: I don't think you've ever mentioned an Uncle Thaddeus before, have you?

LANCE: No, but you've heard of him. (*Sebastian looks confused. Lance, prompting—*) Thaddeus Montgomery?

SEBASTIAN: Thaddeus *P.* Montgomery? The famous industrialist?

LANCE: That's the one.

SEBASTIAN: You mean to tell me your uncle is Thaddeus P. Montgomery and we're forced to live like this?

He makes a gesture indicting the apartment.

LANCE: I wouldn't ask him for money. My cousin Richard tried it once.

SEBASTIAN: What happened?

LANCE: Uncle Thaddeus hired a team of lawyers and had him legally removed from the family.

SEBASTIAN: Sounds like a tough man.

LANCE: He is.

SEBASTIAN: Didn't he get called before a Congressional committee a few months ago? Something about corporate tax evasion?

LANCE: That's right. He's the president of sixteen major companies, none of which has ever paid any taxes.

SEBASTIAN: How does he get away with it?

LANCE: He juggles the books so that none of the companies ever show any profits.

SEBASTIAN (*as if it's almost too much to believe*): And he's *your* uncle?

LANCE: Yeah. (*He looks wistfully into the distance.*) I think he's always been kind of disappointed in me. (*He turns to Sebastian.*) Every time I see him, he tells me that the true worth of a man is measured by his money-making ability.

SEBASTIAN: That's sounds pretty funny coming from a man who runs sixteen non-profit organizations.

Lance smiles at this, then starts to read the letter again.

LANCE: Oh, no!

SEBASTIAN: What's wrong?

LANCE (*looking at his watch*): He's flying in tonight at eight o'clock and wants me to meet him at the airport.

SEBASTIAN: You can make it.

LANCE: Just barely. I have to change clothes and then take a cab over there and find out what terminal he's coming in at. (*He starts to unbutton his shirt and heads for the bedrooms. He grumbles*—) Next time you have to funnel some milk, I wish you'd use your own mail. (*He suddenly stops dead. Then he turns to Sebastian and moans*—) Oh, Sebastian. My uncle isn't going to understand the way we live. He isn't going to understand it at all.

SEBASTIAN: What's wrong with the way we live?

LANCE: Everything. Normal people don't have human specimens lying around, and normal people don't treat other people like guinea pigs. Please, Sebastian, don't perform any experiments while my uncle's here.

SEBASTIAN (*reluctantly*): Okay.

LANCE: And don't bring any specimens home.

SEBASTIAN: All right.

LANCE (*looking at the body*): And we have to do something about this guy.

SEBASTIAN: I could put some potted plants around him.

LANCE (*desperately*): Sebastian . . .

SEBASTIAN: Don't worry, I'll take care of it. You just get changed and get to the airport.

LANCE: Okay.

He exits to the bedrooms. Sebastian leans back against his desk and contemplates.

SEBASTIAN (*rubbing his hands together*): Thaddeus P. Montgomery. What a specimen!

Curtain

ACT TWO

Scene One

Same scene as before, several hours later. Sebastian sits reading on the couch. The specimen is still on the floor. Lance enters in a state of excitement.

LANCE: Sebastian, are you— Hey, you were supposed to get rid of that guy.

Sebastian looks over his book at the body.

SEBASTIAN: Oh, is he still here? I told him to leave.

LANCE: This isn't funny, Sebastian. My uncle's on his way up here right now. He just stopped to yell at his valet.

SEBASTIAN: He brought a valet?

LANCE: Yes, and they'll both be up here any second.

SEBASTIAN: I've never met a real valet before.

LANCE: Come on, Sebastian. We can't let my uncle find your specimen up here.

SEBASTIAN: We could pitch him out the window.

LANCE: I'm not going to pitch this guy out the window.

SEBASTIAN: I meant your uncle.

LANCE: Be serious, Sebastian. We don't have much time.

SEBASTIAN: Okay, let's carry my specimen downstairs and lay him in the gutter.

LANCE: No.

SEBASTIAN: Why not? He'll look perfectly natural.

LANCE: I'm sure. But my uncle's right at the bottom of the stairs. We'd never get this guy past him.

SEBASTIAN: Then we'll have to hide him here in the apartment.

LANCE: Where?

SEBASTIAN: How about in one of the bedrooms?

LANCE: No, he'd find him in there.

SEBASTIAN: The coat closet?

LANCE: He'd find him in there.

SEBASTIAN: You pick a place.

Lance thinks hard.

LANCE: We'll hide him in the coat closet.

SEBASTIAN: Good plan.

LANCE: We just have to remember to keep my uncle out of there until we can sneak this guy out.

SEBASTIAN: Okay, you get his legs. I'll get this end.

They start to transport the specimen.

LANCE: I had no idea he'd be this heavy.

SEBASTIAN: I had to have two people help me drag him up here.

LANCE: Next time, why don't you get a specimen that can walk?

SEBASTIAN: I didn't know I'd have to play hide-and-seek with him. (*They reach the door.*) Here, set him down. (*Sebastian reaches back, opens the door, then grabs the body again.*) Okay, lift. (*He backs into the closet and abruptly stops when he hits the back wall.*) This is no good. Pull him out.

They drag him out of the closet.

LANCE (*desperately*): Hurry.

SEBASTIAN: Let's see: if he won't fit horizontally, let's try vertically. (*They struggle to stand him up.*) Lift. (*They lift him. Sebastian attaches the neck of his coat to a coat hook in the door.)* There. Now let's get his feet out of the way. (*He lifts the specimen's feet and sets them on a shoe rack which is attached to the bottom of the door. He is now hanging so that he swings with the door as it is opened and closed.*) That should do it.

LANCE (*nervously*): Good. Let's just remember to keep my uncle out of there.

SEBASTIAN: Calm down, Lance. You're too tense.

LANCE: Of course I'm tense! I just came all the way back from the airport with my uncle yelling at me because I got there late and yelling at his valet because he forgot to pack some important papers, and I come in here and find out you've still got your specimen sprawled out on the floor.

SEBASTIAN: Relax. It's all taken care of now.

LANCE: Please, Sebastian, please don't do anything strange while my uncle's here.

SEBASTIAN: Is it really that important to you?

LANCE: Yes.

SEBASTIAN: All right. I'll behave.

LANCE: You mean it?

SEBASTIAN: I mean it. I'll treat him as if he were my own father.

LANCE (*greatly relieved*): Oh, thank you, Sebastian, thank you. You don't know how much I— (*There is a knock at the door.*) That's him.

SEBASTIAN: I'm ready.

Lance goes to the door, then stops uncertainly and looks back.

LANCE: Um . . . Sebastian . . .

SEBASTIAN: What?

LANCE: How did you treat your father?

SEBASTIAN: You'd better open the door. Your uncle's waiting. (*Lance hesitates, then opens it. Thaddeus Montgomery enters, followed closely by his valet, Frederick, who is carrying two suitcases and a briefcase. Sebastian steps up to Thaddeus and holds out his hand.*) Hello, Mr. Montgomery. My name's Sebastian. (*Thaddeus passes him without a glance and walks into the room, looking around with a disapproving gaze. Sebastian is left with his hand sticking out. He stands there a moment, then turns to the valet.*) Here, let me help you with those.

He takes the suitcases.

FREDERICK: Thanks.

SEBASTIAN: My name's Sebastian. What's yours?

FREDERICK: I'm—

THADDEUS: Frederick, take my coat.

FREDERICK (*to Sebastian*): Excuse me. (*He takes the overcoat.*) Where should I put this?

SEBASTIAN: There's a coat closet by the door.

LANCE (*quickly*): I'll take it.

He does. No one is looking in the direction of the closet, so they do not see the body which swings into view as Lance hangs the coat.

THADDEUS: This place is revolting. I expected it to be bad, but not like this.

LANCE: Well, it's the best I can afford on my salary.

THADDEUS (*looking around*): You have bugs, I assume?

SEBASTIAN: No, they're real good about that here. An exterminator comes in once a month and kills everything that moves.

THADDEUS: Terrific.

SEBASTIAN: Of course, it's a little hard to breathe

around here for a couple of days after that, but it's worth it not to have bugs crawling all over you.

THADDEUS: Perhaps I should have stayed at a hotel.

SEBASTIAN (*speaking cheerfully*): Nonsense. I'm sure you'll feel right at home here. It's been weeks since they sprayed.

LANCE: Um, Uncle Thaddeus, this my roommate, Sebastian Dumas.

Thaddeus gives Sebastian the same look he has given the room, then turns back to Lance.

THADDEUS: We met at the door. (*turns to Lance*) Where can I set out my papers?

LANCE: Right here on the coffee table. Why don't you sit down and make yourself comfortable?

Thaddeus looks dubiously at the couch, then sits.

THADDEUS: I'm going to need this table cleared off. Frederick, bring my briefcase over here.

Lance starts clearing the table as Frederick brings the case. Thaddeus opens it and takes out a stack of papers. Frederick positions himself beside the couch in a military stance of attention.

LANCE: Would you like to sit down, Frederick?

THADDEUS: Frederick never sits.

SEBASTIAN: That must get awfully tiring. I guess you just prop him up against something at night, huh?

Frederick starts to chuckle but chokes it off.

THADDEUS (*severely*): *Frederick.*

FREDERICK: Sorry, sir. Just my levity slipping out.

THADDEUS (*to Lance and Sebastian*): He has the bad habit sometimes of finding things amusing.

SEBASTIAN (*indignant*): You should have him flogged.

LANCE (*quickly*): Sebastian, why don't you get my uncle something to drink?

THADDEUS: Frederick will see to that. Frederick.

FREDERICK (*to Sebastian*): Where do you keep your liquor?

SEBASTIAN: Under the cabinet over there.

Frederick goes to the kitchen area and starts making the drink.

THADDEUS: Lance, go down to the car and get the rest

of my luggage. (*to Sebastian*) You, take those suitcases into my room and turn my bed down. I intend to retire early.

Sebastian starts to answer, but Lance pleads with him silently. He relents.

SEBASTIAN: All right.

Sebastian takes the suitcases back to the bedrooms. Lance exits. Thaddeus takes out his cell phone and dials.

THADDEUS: Hello, Jack? Montgomery here. . . . I just arrived at my nephew's apartment. . . . That's right. I'll be here all weekend. If anything important comes up, call me immediately. . . . No, I have to call Murchison tonight and check the figures. That Kingston crowd is pushing hard on this one. They just might have the low bid. (*Frederick hands him the drink. He sips, then hands it back to Frederick angrily.*) There's too much water in this. Fix it. (*speaks into the phone*) Yes, I got the contracts all signed. Sullivan tried to hold out, but when I threatened to go with Allied Aluminum, he gave in. . . . Okay, I'll call you tomorrow just after the bids. . . . All right. . . . Goodbye. (*He hangs up. Frederick hands him his drink, then stands at attention again. Sebastian enters from the bedroom. Thaddeus looks through the papers in his briefcase.*) Where's the sheet with the steel figures? You didn't forget to pack that, too, did you?

FREDERICK: No, sir. It's in one of the suitcases your nephew is getting.

THADDEUS: Well, why isn't he back yet?

SEBASTIAN: Was there anything valuable in your luggage?

THADDEUS: Why?

SEBASTIAN: Oh, I don't know. It's just that there's a pawn shop next door . . .

He lets his words trail off. Thaddeus looks at him curiously, as if trying to determine whether Sebastian is putting him on. Then Lance enters.

FREDERICK: Here he is.

THADDEUS: Which case is it in?

FREDERICK: The brown one, sir.

THADDEUS: Get it.

Frederick takes the brown case from Lance, opens it, and retrieves the sheet with the steel figures. Sebastian sits next to Thaddeus on the couch and picks up some papers Thaddeus had laid out on the table.

SEBASTIAN: These look interesting. What are they?

THADDEUS (*grabbing them away from him*): Keep your hands off my papers.

SEBASTIAN *(rising):* Sorry. (*He goes to the kitchen area.*) Lance, you want something to drink?

LANCE: No, thanks.

SEBASTIAN: Frederick? (*Frederick looks at Thaddeus. Thaddeus looks back sternly. Frederick turns to Sebastian and shakes his head.*) I see. Frederick doesn't drink, either.

Sebastian retrieves a bottle of water from the refrigerator and opens it as Thaddeus dials his phone again. Sebastian sips.

THADDEUS (*into phone*): Thaddeus Montgomery here. Let me talk to Bill Murchison. . . . Then wake him up. (*He drums his fingers on the table while he waits.*) Hello, Murchison? . . . I got those contracts signed, but I need to check some figures. Do you have your WDY report? . . . Okay, I'll wait. (*He drums his fingers and looks around the room.)* I suppose welfare pays for this place?

LANCE: No, sir. I have a job.

THADDEUS: Last time I spoke to your father, he said you didn't.

LANCE: I had a little trouble finding something when I first came here, but I'm working now.

THADDEUS: Where?

LANCE: The Food Mart. It's a great place to work. The

people are—

THADDEUS (*abruptly, into the phone*): Got it? . . . Right. I want you to check the price on those beams. (*He pulls a pen from his shirt pocket and begins to write.*) Uh, huh. Does that include installation? . . . Okay, check the figures on that concrete. . . . No, it's on the other sheet. . . . Well, be quick about it. (*He drums his fingers.*) What position do you hold?

LANCE: What? Oh, I work in the produce department.

THADDEUS: You mean you wash vegetables for a living?

LANCE (*defensively*): I also stack 'em.

THADDEUS (*into phone*): No, that's not right. I have a hundred and thirty over sixty-five. Add it up again. (*to Lance*) When I was your age, I was already making over a hundred thousand a year and beginning to invest in the stock market. (*into phone*) Yes, that's right. Now remember: call me first thing in the morning. . . . Yes, as soon as they open the bids. I'm sure we can beat those that are already sealed, but I want to hear Kingston's bid as soon as you have it. . . . All right. Goodbye.

He hangs up and begins making calculations on a slip of paper. Lance tries to start a conversation.

LANCE: So, Uncle Thaddeus, did you have a nice trip?

THADDEUS: Not especially.

LANCE: You didn't mention in your letter that you were bringing a valet. I guess he can have my bed.

THADDEUS: Frederick can sleep on the floor.

LANCE: That's really not necessary. We have several cots.

THADDEUS (*testily*): Are you going to continue this inane chatter all night?

LANCE (*abashed*): No, sir..

THADDEUS: Good. (*He continues to make his calculations, then he stops and looks at Lance.*) Do you have a restroom, or do you have to go down the hall somewhere?

LANCE: No, sir. We have our own restroom.

Pause.

THADDEUS: It wasn't a rhetorical question.

LANCE: Oh, I'm sorry. It's right through there. Let me show you.

THADDEUS: I can find it myself.

He exits, Right.

FREDERICK (*collapsing onto the couch*): Whew!

SEBASTIAN: He's a real charmer.

Frederick takes off one of his shoes and begins to massage his foot.

FREDERICK: You know he makes me stand wherever we go?

SEBASTIAN: It must have been embarrassing on the plane out here.

FREDERICK (*smiling, he stands and holds out his hand*): Say, we really didn't get a chance to meet before. I'm Frederick Lucius Throckmorton.

SEBASTIAN: Frederick Lucius Throckmorton?

FREDERICK: You can call me Joe.

SEBASTIAN: Pleased to meet you, Joe. I'm Sebastian, and this is my roommate, Lance.

FREDERICK: Yes, we met at the airport.

SEBASTIAN: So tell me, Joe, how long have you been working for—

FREDERICK: Um, excuse me, do you mind if I sit down?

SEBASTIAN: No, go right ahead.

FREDERICK: Thanks. (*He sits.*) I didn't mean to be rude. It's just that Mr. Montgomery will only be out of the room a few minutes, and I don't want to waste any time standing around.

SEBASTIAN: I understand.

FREDERICK: Now, you were saying?

SEBASTIAN: I just wondered how long you've been working for Lance's uncle.

FREDERICK: Oh, ages. At least six month.

SEBASTIAN: That's ages?

LANCE: It is for one of my uncle's valets. They usually don't last for more than a month and a half.

FREDERICK: It's because of the way he treats us. You may not have noticed, but my job is kind of demeaning.

SEBASTIAN: Why don't you quit?

FREDERICK: Oh, I'm learning a lot from Mr. Montgomery. Someday I want to be a wealthy businessman just like him, so I view my being his valet as sort of an apprenticeship. He's just like the great robber barons of old. I've never known a man more vile or corrupt. (*to Lance*) No offense.

Lance indicates no offense was taken.

SEBASTIAN: Do you mind if I ask you a personal question, Joe?

FREDERICK: No, what?

SEBASTIAN: It's about your name. I've been sitting here turning it over in my mind again and again—Frederick Lucius Throckmorton—and I just don't see how you get "Joe" out of that.

FREDERICK: Oh, well, Joe is my real name, but I've always aspired to something higher. People named Joe never get anywhere. You have to have a name like Cornelius Vanderbilt, J. Pierpont Morgan . . .

SEBASTIAN: Thaddeus P. Montgomery.

FREDERICK: Exactly. So when I decided it was time for me to make my way in the world, I chose a name I was sure would rise. (*grandly*) Frederick Lucius Throckmorton. (*proudly*) You can almost see orphans being turned out of their homes. (*There is a brief pause as he looks dreamily into space in happy contemplation of his name. He then turns to Sebastian.*) Someday I hope to make the name of Throckmorton one of the most reviled in the nation.

SEBASTIAN: That's quite a goal.

FREDERICK: Yes. So you can see why I don't quit my job, even though—

He is interrupted by a knock at the door.

SEBASTIAN (*calling*): It's open.

Enter Lisa Dumas. She is carrying several shopping bags.

LISA: Hi, guys.

SEBASTIAN: Oh, Lisa, come on in.

LISA (*setting down the bags*): I can only stay a minute because I— (*Frederick looks at her and quickly rises.*) Oh, hello.

FREDERICK (*almost stuttering, he obviously finds her attractive*): Hi. I'm Joe . . . Fred . . . Frederick.

LISA (*smiling, holds out her hand*): Hello, Joe Fred Frederick. I'm Lisa Dumas.

He holds out the hand with the shoe, then quickly shoves it under his arm and shakes hands with her.

SEBASTIAN: Joe is his real name. Fred Frederick is just an alias.

LISA: I see. Are you Sebastian's latest specimen?

FREDERICK: Sebastian's . . . ? Uh, no, I'm Mr. Montgomery's valet.

LISA (*looks at Lance*): Since when have you had a valet?

LANCE: No, he belongs to my uncle.

Lisa looks confused.

SEBASTIAN: Lance's uncle is spending the weekend here, and Fred Frederick is his valet.

FREDERICK: Call me Joe.

LISA: All right. I'm pleased to meet you, Joe.

FREDERICK: So am I. I mean, I, you. You know?

LISA (*smiling*): I know.

FREDERICK: Listen, I'm going to be in town all weekend. Maybe you and I could—

He is cut off by Thaddeus' abrupt entry.

THADDEUS: That bathroom is disgusting. (*He heads for the couch.*) I hope I don't get a staph infection while I'm here.

He picks up his calculator and starts working.

LISA (*to Lance*): Is this your uncle? (*Lance nods.*) Hello, Mr. Montgomery. I'm Lisa Dumas. I—

THADDEUS (*vehemently*): Sshhh!

LISA: Oh, I'm sorry. I'll wait until you—

THADDEUS: Shut up! (*Sebastian rises. Lisa puts her hands on his chest and shakes her head. Thaddeus works a moment longer, then lays down his calculator, rises, and looks at Lance.*) I'm going to leave these contracts here on the table. I trust they won't be disturbed. (*to Frederick*) Frederick, I expect to be awakened by seven o'clock, sharp.

FREDERICK: Yes, sir.

THADDEUS (*to Lance*): For breakfast I'll have bacon, eggs, toast, and orange juice. Can you remember that? (*Lance nods.*) Fine. I'll see you in the morning.

He starts to exit.

LANCE: Wait, Uncle Thaddeus. You haven't met Sebastian's sister, yet.

Thaddeus lets out a deep sigh of resignation, turns to face Lisa, and crosses his arms. Several moments pass.

THADDEUS (*as though from a great height*): Well?

LISA (*awkwardly*): Um, I'm very pleased to meet you, Mr. Montgomery. (*pause*) I'm Lisa Dumas.

Thaddeus looks at her a moment without answering, then turns to Lance.

THADDEUS: Is that it? Good. I'll be going to bed, then. (*to Sebastian, sarcastically*) Unless you have some other relatives you'd like me to meet. (*to Frederick*) Remember, I want to be up by seven.

FREDERICK: Yes, sir.

Thaddeus exits. There is an awkward pause.

LANCE: I'm sorry, Lisa. It's just his way.

LISA: Don't worry about it. I'm sure he didn't mean to be rude. I just interrupted him while he was trying to think. I'll come by tomorrow after work and—Oh . . . (*She looks at her watch.*) I really need to be going. It was nice meeting you, Joe. I hope I see you again before you leave town.

FREDERICK: Why don't you let me drive you home? We have a rental car downstairs.

LISA: You don't have to bother. I can just catch a cab.

FREDERICK: But I want to.

LISA: Okay. That'll be nice.

FREDERICK: Let me get your bags.

LISA: Thank you. (*They start toward the door. Lisa turns to Sebastian and Lance.*) Goodbye, you two.

SEBASTIAN: Goodbye, Lisa.

LANCE: Bye.

Lisa exits.

FREDERICK: Don't wait up for me.

SEBASTIAN (*sternly*): That's my sister.

FREDERICK (*deflated*): I'll be right back.

He exits. There is a pause. Sebastian is looking in the direction of the bedroom door where Thaddeus exited a few moments earlier.

LANCE: Sebastian?

SEBASTIAN: Hmmm?

LANCE: Will you be going to bed soon?

SEBASTIAN: Pretty soon. I just want to straighten up a little and put out the trash.

LANCE: Oh, okay. (*He heads for the hallway.*) Good night.

SEBASTIAN: Good night.

Lance exits. Sebastian goes behind the kitchen counter and picks up a trash sack which is about half full. He grabs some soda cans and paper plates which are on the counter and drops them in, then goes to his desk and clears it of some of its debris. Finally he goes to the table in front of the couch and picks up the contracts, one by one, tossing them into the bag. When the table is cleared, he turns Upstage and strolls out of the apartment, whistling a little tune.

Blackout

ACT TWO

Scene Two

Same scene as before, early the next morning. Sebastian is up, dressed, and preparing breakfast. There's a knock at the door.

SEBASTIAN: It's open. (*Enter Lisa Dumas.*) Hi. I wasn't expecting to see *you* this morning.

LISA: I just stopped by on my way to work.

SEBASTIAN: You have time for breakfast?

LISA: Sure.

SEBASTIAN: Have a seat. I'll get you a cup of coffee.

She sits and watches him pour. Her face and manner indicate she's struggling with some thought.

LISA (*uncertainly*): Say, Bass . . .

SEBASTIAN: Mmmm?

LISA: After I went home last night, I got to thinking.

SEBASTIAN: We Dumas are famous for that.

LISA: That's not all we're famous for.

SEBASTIAN: Meaning?

LISA: I know you, Bass. I think you're going to pull something on Lance's uncle for being rude to me last night.

SEBASTIAN: What makes you think I'd want to pull something on Mr. Montgomery, just because he's a pompous, obnoxious . . .

LISA: Bass . . .

SEBASTIAN: You shouldn't worry so much about the bad things that might happen to people. It'll keep you awake nights. (*She starts to answer, but he cuts her off.*) Look, I've spent years studying the human animal, and one thing I've learned is: most people eventually get what they deserve in this life.

LISA: But it doesn't always have to be you who gives it to them..

SEBASTIAN: Well, if you're really all that worried about Mr. Montgomery, you could—Oh, hello, Joe.

Frederick has just entered from the bedroom. He's wearing his uniform pants and dress shirt but not his uniform coat. Lisa turns to look at him.

FREDERICK: Good morning.

LISA: Good morning, Joe.

SEBASTIAN: Would you like some breakfast?

FREDERICK: I'm not allowed to eat in the morning. Mr. Montgomery says it will make me fat and lazy.

SEBASTIAN: Surely you can sneak a couple of eggs or perhaps a slice of bacon while he's not looking.

FREDERICK: I guess a little breakfast wouldn't hurt just this once.

SEBASTIAN: Sure. (*Frederick sits beside Lisa at the counter.*) Oh, I didn't mean here. I meant you should take my sister out for breakfast.

FREDERICK (*confused*): Oh, I just thought . . .

He motions to what Sebastian is cooking.

SEBASTIAN: No, Mr. Montgomery might catch you if you try to eat something here. You really should go out.

FREDERICK (*to Lisa*): I'm game if you are. Unless it would make you late for work.

LISA: No, I don't have to be there until nine.

FREDERICK: Great.

LISA: I'm not sure it's such a good idea, though. You leaving, I mean. Mr. Montgomery might need you for something.

FREDERICK (*turning to Sebastian*): You can take care of Mr. Montgomery until I get back, can't you?

SEBASTIAN: As a matter of fact, I was promising Lisa that very thing when you came in.

FREDERICK (*to Lisa*): And I'll only be gone about an hour. What could happen in that length of time?

LISA (*looking at Sebastian*): That's what I'm wondering.

FREDERICK (*disappointed*): Of course, if you don't want to . . .

LISA: No, I'd like to. It's just—

SEBASTIAN: It's all settled then. You two go have a good time, and I'll take care of Mr. Montgomery.

LISA: Bass . . .

SEBASTIAN: Really. It'll be all right.

LISA (*still uncertain, she turns to Frederick):* Okay. I'd love to.

FREDERICK: Great. (*They start to exit.*) Thanks a lot,

Sebastian. I'll try not to be too long.

SEBASTIAN: Take your time.

FREDERICK: Thanks.

Frederick and Lisa exit. Sebastian starts whistling as he goes back to the stove. Lance enters, buttoning his shirt.

SEBASTIAN: Good morning.

LANCE: Isn't it kind of early for you to be up?

SEBASTIAN: Not really. Your uncle said he wanted his breakfast promptly at seven, and it's almost that now.

LANCE: You're fixing it yourself?

SEBASTIAN: Sure.

LANCE: But you don't even make your own breakfast.

SEBASTIAN: This is a special occasion. It's not every day we have a man like your uncle staying with us.

Lance sits on one of the stools at the kitchen counter.

LANCE: I was afraid you'd be mad at him for the way he treated your sister, but you're really being great.

SEBASTIAN (*modestly*): Oh, well . . .

LANCE: No, I mean it. Fixing him breakfast and all.

SEBASTIAN: You'd do the same for me if I had a rich uncle.

LANCE: Anyway, I appreciate it.

SEBASTIAN: Sure. You want some breakfast?

LANCE: No, thanks. You know breakfast always sets a little heavy with me.

SEBASTIAN: Yeah.

LANCE: That bacon smells good, though. What else are you making?

SEBASTIAN: Everything the man asked for: eggs, toast, juice . . .

LANCE: Have you bought a paper yet?

SEBASTIAN: Not yet.

LANCE: I think I'll run down and get one. Will you wake my uncle for me?

SEBASTIAN: Sure.

Lance exits. Sebastian reaches under the counter and grabs two large metal pots, then goes to the hallway. He rapidly begins to bang the pots together.

SEBASTIAN (*shouting*): Fire! Fire! Save yourselves! The building's on fire! Run for your lives! Fire! Fire!

Thaddeus comes running out of the bedroom, awkwardly trying to put on his bathrobe as he runs. As soon as he appears, Sebastian stops hitting the pots together and stands there, calmly and quietly. Thaddeus passes him on the way to the door, then stops and looks back.

THADDEUS: What—what's going on?

SEBASTIAN: You said you wanted to be awakened by seven.

THADDEUS: But I didn't mean that I wanted—

SEBASTIAN: This is how we always get up around here.

THADDEUS: Always?

SEBASTIAN: Every morning.

THADDEUS (*grabbing his head*): Doesn't it leave you kind of addled?

SEBASTIAN: Sometimes.

THADDEUS: I'd rather be awakened by gunshots.

SEBASTIAN: I'll remember that for in the morning.

Sebastian returns to the kitchen area.

THADDEUS (*following him*): No, wait. I just meant—

SEBASTIAN: How do you want your eggs, Uncle Thaddeus?

THADDEUS: Oh, uh, scrambled. And it's Mr. Montgomery to you.

SEBASTIAN: If you'll just have a seat there, your breakfast will be ready in a second.

Thaddeus pulls out his cell phone and checks for messages. He looks around.

THADDEUS: Where's Frederick? I need him to lay out my clothes.

SEBASTIAN: I gave him the day off.

THADDEUS: What? He knows better than that. He doesn't get any days off.

SEBASTIAN: Maybe that's why he accepted so eagerly. Anyway, Lance and I will be here if you need anything.

THADDEUS (*grumbling*): I've got a good mind to . . . (*looks abruptly at Sebastian*) How much longer is breakfast going to be? I'm used to eating as soon as I get up.

SEBASTIAN: It'll just be a few more minutes.

Thaddeus looks across at the pan where Sebastian is cooking.

THADDEUS: You sure aren't making very much.

SEBASTIAN: This is just for you. Lance never eats breakfast, and I've already had mine. If you're hungry, you can start on this.

He hands him a plate with several pieces of toast. Thaddeus picks one up.

THADDEUS: Why does this toast look so funny?

SEBASTIAN: It looks fine to me.

THADDEUS (*sniffing it*): It smells kind of strange, too.

SEBASTIAN: Taste it.

THADDEUS (*taking a bite*): This is awful. What's wrong with it?

SEBASTIAN: Nothing.

THADDEUS: Don't give me that. I've been eating toast all my life. This doesn't even feel right.

SEBASTIAN: Well, since Lance works at the Food Mart, they give us a special on anything that starts to spoil or form mold.

Thaddeus drops the toast and shudders.

THADDEUS: Unngghh. Give me something to drink, quick. (*Sebastian hands him a glass of milk. Thaddeus drinks and immediately spits it back into the glass.*) Something that's not spoiled, you idiot!

Sebastian gets him a glass of water from the tap. Thaddeus drinks it down, then rises and heads for the bedrooms.

SEBASTIAN: Where are you going? Your eggs are almost ready.

THADDEUS: Forget it.

SEBASTIAN: But—

THADDEUS: I said, forget it. I have some important deals coming up in the next few days, and I can't afford to get botulism!

He exits. Lance enters with the paper.

LANCE: Is my uncle up?

SEBASTIAN: Yes. I think he's getting dressed. He decided not to eat breakfast.

LANCE: Really? That doesn't sound like him.

Lance goes to the couch, sits, and opens the paper.

SEBASTIAN: Well, he ate a little toast. (*He scrapes the eggs onto a plate.*) No sense letting good eggs go to waste. (*He comes around the counter and sits in one of the living room chairs. He begins to eat the eggs.*) Anything interesting in the paper?

LANCE: No. Same old stuff.

SEBASTIAN: Let me see the editorial section.

LANCE: Okay. (*He digs it out.*) There you go.

Sebastian begins to read. Thaddeus enters. He has on his pants and shoes and is carrying his shirt.

LANCE: Good morning, Uncle Thaddeus. Did you sleep well?

THADDEUS (*putting on his shirt*): I did not. I don't see how anyone can sleep on those torture boards you call beds. I was up all night.

LANCE: I'm sorry.

THADDEUS (*moving to the couch*): I really think it might be a good idea if I went to a hotel.

SEBASTIAN (*pleasantly*): You can't do that, Uncle Thaddeus. Think of all the fun we're going to have this weekend.

THADDEUS: I told you not to call me that. (*He reaches for where his contracts should be on the table, then stops when he sees they're not there. He starts to open his briefcase.*) Call me Mr. Montgomery if you find it necessary to speak to me at all. And as for having fun this weekend . . . (*His words trail off as he discovers his briefcase empty. He looks on the table again, then looks quickly around on the floor.*) Hey, where are my contracts?

SEBASTIAN (*innocently*): Contracts?

THADDEUS: The papers I had on this table. They're gone.

SEBASTIAN: Oh, those. I thought they were just scrap paper.

THADDEUS: What did you do with them?

SEBASTIAN: I threw them out.

THADDEUS: Threw them out?! Those contracts were worth a quarter of a billion dollars!

SEBASTIAN: Well, what's a quarter of a billion dollars, more or less?

THADDEUS: I don't have time to stand around listening to your atheistic spoutings! Just show me where my contracts are!

SEBASTIAN: I put them in the trash bin outside the door. (*Thaddeus heads for the door.*) But you won't find them there.

THADDEUS (*stops*): Why not?

SEBASTIAN: I heard the building superintendent come by several minutes ago and get the trash.

THADDEUS: Where would he have taken it?

SEBASTIAN: Down to the basement to burn it, most likely.

THADDEUS: Quick! Take me there! We've got to stop him!

SEBASTIAN: But I haven't finished eating my eggs.

THADDEUS: Forget the eggs, you dimwit! My contracts are probably going up in smoke right this minute!!!

LANCE: I'll take you down there, Uncle Thaddeus.

THADDEUS (*rushing to the door*): Well, come on, hurry up!

Thaddeus and Lance exit.

SEBASTIAN: That poor man's liable to burst a vessel. (*He rises, goes to the kitchen area, and scrapes the rest of his eggs into the sink. Thaddeus' cell phone rings. He goes and picks it up.*) Hello . . . Thaddeus Montgomery? No, I'm sorry. He was killed in an automobile accident this morning. . . . You can attend the memorial dance they're having at the Plaza tonight, though . . . His family? No, I'm afraid you couldn't speak with them. . . . Yes, they left this morning for a tour of Europe. . . . Sudden? Yes, but they had just come into a great deal of money. . . . Yes . . . (*There is a knock at the door.*) I'm sorry, I have to go. Someone's at the door. Probably another well-wisher . . . No, no bother at all. (*He hangs up and goes to the door. Mrs. Vail enters.*) Ah, Mrs. Vail. I'm glad you came.

VAIL: On the phone you said it was urgent. Has your roommate gone out of control again?

SEBASTIAN: No, nothing like that. I just need you to do me a favor. (*She turns and heads for the door.*) Wait, at least hear me out. It's very important.

Mrs. Vail stops and turns.

VAIL: You have two minutes.

SEBASTIAN: Thank you. Let's see, how should I begin? Well, as you may or may not know, Lance's uncle—Thaddeus Montgomery—is staying with us for a few days. Perhaps you've heard of him?

VAIL: No.

SEBASTIAN: Well, anyway, Mr. Montgomery is an extremely rich man, and he—

VAIL (*with sudden interest*): He's rich?

SEBASTIAN: Extremely.

Mrs. Vail comes a little closer, wanting to hear more.

VAIL: Go on.

SEBASTIAN: As I was saying, Mr. Montgomery is going to be spending a few days with us, and I want his stay here to be as pleasant as possible. In fact, he's promised that if he has a good time here, he'll reward Lance and me handsomely. Any money he gave us, we'd be glad to split with you.

VAIL (*trying to pretend indifference*): I might be willing to help. What exactly would that entail?

SEBASTIAN: Well, how shall I put this? I have a bit of a problem. You see, I don't know many women in your . . . um . . . age group, and I was wondering if you knew any women who might, well, to be frank with you, I wanted to know if you might have any friends who might want to date Mr. Montgomery while he's in town.

VAIL: Date him?

SEBASTIAN: Yes.

VAIL (*firmly*): Mr. Dumas, I know only nice women.

SEBASTIAN: And it's nice women I'm talking about. Mr. Montgomery is not looking for pleasure. He's looking for a wife. But he has trouble finding women to date. You see, he's been hurt so many times. Mr. Montgomery is generous to a fault; practically throws away his money on the women he goes out with, buying them expensive jewelry and cars. But do they appreciate it? No. Everywhere he goes, it's the same thing. Greedy women try to lure him into their snares. They pretend to be in love with him just to get their hands on his fabulous wealth.

VAIL (*hypocritically*): That's terrible.

SEBASTIAN: Yes. It's left Mr. Montgomery a broken man. In spite of his extreme wealth, he's terribly lonely.

VAIL: The poor, dear man.

SEBASTIAN: Why, if he met a woman who could love him for himself and show him that she understands, that she knows what it is to be lonely, he'd probably marry her on the spot and throw all his riches at her feet.

VAIL: Just exactly how rich *is* Mr. Montgomery?

SEBASTIAN: He owns sixteen different companies, none of which has ever paid a penny of tax.

VAIL: Wow.

SEBASTIAN: And the sad thing is, with his health as bad as it is, he's not expected to live very long. If he doesn't find someone soon, he'll die a lonely, embittered man with no one to leave his money to.

VAIL: That's so sad.

SEBASTIAN: Yes. So do you think you can help me? Do you think any of your friends might be willing to date this kind, generous, dying man?

VAIL: I don't see why it necessarily has to be a friend. I was thinking maybe—

The door bursts open and Thaddeus storms in carrying papers which have been crumpled and are stained with tomato juice, coffee grounds, etc. He looks as if he's been in a scuffle. Thaddeus heads for the couch as Lance follows him into the apartment.

THADDEUS: Imagine the nerve of that imbecile, telling me it was against the law to let someone go through other people's trash! Well, I showed him. (*Mrs. Vail looks inquiringly at Sebastian who point to Thaddeus, nods, and mouths "That's him." Mrs. Vail goes to the couch and sits next to Thaddeus. Thaddeus looks up at Sebastian.*) Did my cell phone ring while I was gone?

SEBASTIAN: Not that I noticed.

THADDEUS (*checks watch*): He should have called by now. (*He begins straightening out the contracts and picking bits of garbage off them.*) These look awful. Fortunately, you can still make out the signatures.

Mrs. Vail clears her throat. No one notices. She clears it again, violently this time. Thaddeus looks over, startled.

LANCE: Oh, I'm sorry. Uncle Thaddeus, this is Mrs. Vail. Mrs. Vail, my Uncle Thaddeus.

VAIL: I'm a widow.

THADDEUS: Congratulations.

SEBASTIAN: Mrs. Vail has buried three husbands, although we suspect the third one was faking.

VAIL: I own this apartment building. I'm a very business-minded woman.

THADDEUS (*as if he could not possibly care less*): That's very interesting. (*He looks at his watch again.*) Are you sure my cell phone never rang? That doesn't make sense. Maybe I'd better call in to make certain. (*He picks up the phone and dials.*) Let me speak to Bill Murchison. . . . I don't care if he *is* on the other line. Tell him it's Thaddeus

Montgomery. . . . What?! Now see here, woman . . . (*He looks shocked.*) She hung up on me. That fool woman told me I was dead and then hung up on me! Well, we'll see about that! (*He dials again.*) Now, listen here, you . . . (*He's shocked once more.*) She did it again! (*He dials one last time. This time he disguises his voice.*) Hello. This is Chester Adams. May I speak to Mr. Murchison, please? . . . Yes, I'll hold. (*He puts his hand over the receiver and speaks to the room at large.*) Imagine, telling me I'm dead and then hanging up on me. I'll have that idiot-woman fired. I'll—(*into the phone*) Murchison, what in the name of Jim Fisk is going on down there? Every time I call, your secretary hangs up on me! . . . Thaddeus Montgomery. Who do you think? . . . You heard what? . . . What are you running down there, anyway? . . . Never mind, I don't care about that. Just give me the figures on the Davidson deal. . . . What?! What do you mean, Kingston gave the low bid? I haven't given *my* bid yet. . . . But I'm not dead, you idiot! Can't you get that through your iron skull? Listen, Murchison, no, just shut up and listen. I've got something very important to tell you. You're fired! (*He hangs up.*) Can you believe that? They thought I was dead, so they just went ahead without me. (*He starts to stand.*) I've got a good mind to—Ooooh.

He stops and grabs his back and sinks onto the couch, emitting a moan of agony.

LANCE: Uncle Thaddeus, are you all right?

THADDEUS: No, I'm not all right. My back is killing me.

LANCE: What caused it?

THADDEUS: Sleeping on that torture bed and then fighting with that stupid janitor.

LANCE: Maybe you should go lie down.

THADDEUS: On the torture bed? You'd make a great doctor.

He tries to stand and groans again, then sits there rubbing his back.

LANCE: Is there anything I can do?

THADDEUS: No, the pain's almost gone now. It's just a sort of dull ache.

VAIL (*putting her hands on him*): Oh, you poor thing. Would you like me to give you a body massage?

Surprised and somewhat frightened, Thaddeus moves away from her on the couch.

THADDEUS: I would not!

VAIL (*pursuing him*): But if your muscles are sore . . .

THADDEUS (*backing further along the couch*): Get away from me.

VAIL: I just want you to realize I *understand*. (*She corners him at the edge of the couch and places her hands on his chest.*) I *know* what it is to be *lonely*.

THADDEUS (*rising and pushing her away*): I'm sure you do, madam.

Mrs. Vail stands and pursues him around the room.

VAIL: Don't be afraid. I want you for yourself.

THADDEUS: What's the matter with you, woman? Lance, get this person away from me.

VAIL: Don't fight it, Mr. Montgomery. You need the gentle hand of a woman to help you manage your vast fortune. You need a wife who will understand.

THADDEUS: I assure you, I'm a happily unmarried man.

VAIL: No man is happy if he's unmarried.

THADDEUS: I swear to you—Do you have a Bible? I'll say an oath. Lance, do something.

LANCE: Mrs. Vail, maybe it would be better if you—

VAIL: I know how bitter you are. I know how difficult it is for you to trust anyone.

THADDEUS (*in desperation*): Sebastian, help!

Sebastian steps up.

SEBASTIAN: Mrs. Vail, why don't you let Lance get you something to drink while I talk to Mr. Montgomery alone?

VAIL: But—

SEBASTIAN: It'll be all right. Trust me.

VAIL: Okay. (*to Thaddeus*) I'll be right back.

She and Lance go to the kitchen area.

THADDEUS: What's the matter with that woman? Does she behave like this often?

SEBASTIAN: I'm afraid so. It's a sad case. Bad mental problems. Whenever she meets a man who's—well, shall we say, older than most?—she falls madly in love with him and wants to join with him forever. And if he rejects her, and most do, that just makes her want him all the more.

THADDEUS: That's awful.

SEBASTIAN: Yes. The really tragic part is, to make sure that no one else can have her lover, she usually stabs him.

THADDEUS: Stabs him?! Why don't the authorities do anything about it?

SEBASTIAN: She's a distant cousin of the governor. Need I say more?

THADDEUS: But what can I do? I can't just wait around for her to stab me.

SEBASTIAN: No. There's only one thing to do.

THADDEUS: Tell me.

SEBASTIAN: Ask her to marry you.

THADDEUS: What!?!

SEBASTIAN: It's the only way.

THADDEUS: You're as crazy as she is. I'm not about to marry that lunatic.

SEBASTIAN: I don't mean that you should actually marry her. It's just that, for some reason, due to the nature of her illness, when a man asks her to marry him, she loses all interest.

THADDEUS: Really?

SEBASTIAN: Yes.

THADDEUS: Couldn't I get rid of her some other way?

SEBASTIAN: There is no other way.

THADDEUS: Are you sure?

SEBASTIAN: I'm certain.

THADDEUS: There's no other way?

SEBASTIAN: There's no other way.

THADDEUS: All right. Bring her on.

SEBASTIAN: Okay. But don't just blurt it out. It has to sound sincere. Flatter her a little. Apologize for rejecting her earlier. Remember, the nicer you are, the more turned off she'll be. At the slightest sign of repulsion, she'll regain her interest.

THADDEUS: I'll remember.

SEBASTIAN: Okay, good luck. (*calls out*) Mrs. Vail, would you come over here, please? Mr. Montgomery has something he would like to tell you.

VAIL (*eagerly*): Yes, Thaddeus?

THADDEUS: Er, uh, Mrs. Vail . . . (*ahem*) . . . I apologize for the way I was acting before . . . and, uh . . . I realize that you're an attractive woman and you probably have all sorts of *good* traits . . . and it was, uh, like you said, I was, uh, just a little reticent because . . . Well, what I'm really trying to say is . . . um . . . (*blurts*) Will you marry me?

VAIL: Oh, yes-yes-yes!

She jumps and throws her arms around him and kisses him on the mouth. He turns his head to the side and looks desperately at Sebastian. Lance is stunned.

THADDEUS: Hey, I thought—

SEBASTIAN: It doesn't work every time.

VAIL: I'm going to make you so happy. Do you want a big church wedding, or do you think we should elope.

THADDEUS: Now just a minute. I think that—

VAIL: Oh, this is so exciting. And we have so much to do. We have to get blood tests and get the license and—oh—I don't know what else.

THADDEUS: I believe there's been some sort of—

VAIL: Now don't you worry about a thing. I'll make all the arrangements. You call your business associates and whoever else you have to and tell them you're taking a few weeks off for your honeymoon, and I'll run down and start preparing my trousseau.

THADDEUS: Your trousseau! Now look here—

VAIL (*going to the door*): Goodbye, my darling.

She exits. Thaddeus whirls on Sebastian and stands there, trembling in anger, unable to find words sufficiently vehement to express his emotions. Then Lance breaks the silence—

LANCE: Are you really going to marry Mrs. Vail?

THADDEUS: No, I'm not going to marry Mrs. Vail!

LANCE: Then why did you ask her?

THADDEUS: Because you've got an idiot for a roommate!

SEBASTIAN: There's no reason to get so upset.

THADDEUS: That creature expects me to marry it!

SEBASTIAN: It's better than getting stabbed.

THADDEUS: How many times?

SEBASTIAN: What?

THADDEUS: It's better than getting stabbed how many times? Surely you don't just mean once or twice. I'd gladly take one or two stab wounds rather than marry that psychopath!

LANCE: I still don't understand. If you didn't want to marry her, then why—?

THADDEUS: Shut up.

LANCE: But you asked her to—

THADDEUS: I don't want to discuss it.

SEBASTIAN: Isn't it fascinating, Lance—the infinite variety of life? That's why I study human beings instead of plants or rocks. Who could have guessed when your uncle arrived yesterday that before twenty-four hours were out he would have asked Mrs. Vail to marry him.

THADDEUS: I never should have come here. If I had gone to a hotel like I had originally planned, none of this would have happened.

SEBASTIAN: You should view your situation philosophically, Uncle Thaddeus. After all, the reason we make mistakes is so we'll learn from them and make sure something worse doesn't happen to us.

THADDEUS: I've lost two hundred and fifty million dollars today and proposed marriage to an insane woman. There's not a whole lot more that can happen to me. (*There is a knock at the door.*) What now? If it's that woman again, I swear I'll push her down the stairs.

SEBASTIAN (*looking through the peephole*): It's not her.

He opens the door and Mitya enters.

MITYA: Where is he? Oh, there you are!

She rushes over to Lance, throws her arms around him, and starts kissing him all over the face. Sebastian closes the door.

THADDEUS: Who is this girl?

LANCE (*struggling to get free*): She's a friend of Sebastian's.

THADDEUS: She seems to know *you* rather well.

LANCE: We just met yesterday.

THADDEUS: Are all the women around here like this? It's preposterous. If you don't—

He is interrupted by a loud banging at the door.

EDGAR (*from offstage*): Mitya! Are you in there, Mitya?

MITYA (*quietly, with some excitement*): Edgar!

LANCE (*in panic*): Edgar!

THADDEUS: Who's Edgar?

LANCE: Another friend of Sebastian's.

THADDEUS (*to Sebastian*): Are all of your friends mental cases?

SEBASTIAN: Most.

EDGAR (*banging on door*): Open up in there!

MITYA: How romantic. Now you can fight for me.

LANCE (*still struggling*): I don't want to fight for you.

SEBASTIAN: Then you'd better hide. And quickly.

LANCE: Here. Let's hide down here.

He indicates the space behind the kitchen counter.

MITYA: Anything you say, my little anemic cupcake.

They hide. Sebastian opens the door. Edgar storms in.

EDGAR: Where is she?

SEBASTIAN: Whom?

EDGAR: Mitya. She left me a note saying she was coming to see her little frail one.

SEBASTIAN: As you can see, her little frail one isn't here.

EDGAR (*looking around, almost convinced*): Well . . .

SEBASTIAN: Although if I were you, I think I'd check the bedrooms.

EDGAR: The bedrooms? I'll ground that skinny little Romeo to pulp.

He exits to the bedrooms.

THADDEUS: Does this sort of thing go on here all the time?

SEBASTIAN: Sure. Doesn't this sort of thing go on where you live?

THADDEUS (*emphatically*): Never! If I'd had any idea . . .

EDGAR (*coming from the bedrooms*): I guess you were telling the truth. She's not here. I'll go look for her at our headquarters, but if she's not there, I'm coming back up here.

SEBASTIAN: Wait, before you go, I'd like you to meet Lance's uncle.

EDGAR: I haven't got time.

SEBASTIAN: But you don't know who his uncle is. Have you ever heard of Thaddeus P. Montgomery?

EDGAR: No, I—Just a second. Thaddeus P. Montgomery? The corporate swine?

SEBASTIAN: He's the one.

THADDEUS: Now see here—

EDGAR: Are you *the* Thaddeus P. Montgomery?

THADDEUS: I am.

EDGAR: Scourge of the working class? Trampler of human rights? Heartless capitalist scum?

THADDEUS (*proudly*): That's me.

EDGAR (*jerks gun out and aims it at Thaddeus*): Give me one good reason why I shouldn't blow your brains out, you bourgeois capitalist pig?

THADDEUS (*in panic*): You'd spend the rest of your life in jail!

EDGAR (*suddenly calm*): Oh . . . You're right . . . Hmmm . . . (*puts gun away*) I guess I'd better talk it over with Tomás. He'll know what to do.

THADDEUS (*grabbing at any straw*): Yes! Talk it over with Tomás. He'll know what to do.

EDGAR: Now don't you go anywhere.

THADDEUS: Oh, I won't. (*Edgar exits.*) That does it! That does it! I'm getting out of here!

Lance and Mitya come up from behind the counter.

MITYA: Are you *really* Thaddeus P. Montgomery?

THADDEUS: What's it to you?

MITYA: Tomás talks about you all the time. He says there'll never truly be justice in this nation until your bloody carcass is dragged through the streets of Washington.

THADDEUS: That's very interesting. Lance, begin packing my things.

MITYA: He'll be very interested to know you're up here. (*She goes to the door, then looks back at Lance.*) See you later, lover.

Mitya exits.

THADDEUS: Don't just stand there, you idiot! Start packing!

LANCE: But Uncle Thaddeus . . .

THADDEUS: Don't talk to me. I'm getting out of this madhouse.

LANCE: There's really a very funny explanation for all of this.

THADDEUS: Forget the explanation. You get my bags while I get my coat.

LANCE: No, wait—!

Thaddeus opens the closet where the body is hanging and lets out a blood curdling scream.

THADDEUS: Aaaghhh!! He's killed somebody! That lunatic roommate of yours has killed somebody!

LANCE: No, that's just one of his human specimens.

THADDEUS: One of his human specimens! I'm going to the police.

He starts to cross to the door. To do this, he has to cross in front of the specimen.

SPECIMEN: Hey!

THADDEUS (*lurching back*): Aaaghhh!

SPECIMEN: You guys are too noisy for me. I'm going back to the park where it's not so hectic.

He pulls himself loose from where he's hanging and exits.

THADDEUS (*breathing heavily, his legs wobbly*): Oh, my goodness. This is too much. You have maniacs with guns coming in and out of here and bodies that get up and walk away. Call the police for me, Lance. I need to sit down.

LANCE (*helping him to a chair*): Come over here, Uncle Thaddeus. I can explain everything.

THADDEUS (*walks unsteadily to a chair, sits*): I don't want any explanations. I just need a few tranquilizers. Go get me a couple out of my suitcase. They're the green pills in the brown bottle.

Lance starts for the hallway but stops when Sebastian calls to him.

SEBASTIAN: Lance. (*He motions for him to come over. Lance goes over to him and Sebastian pulls a bottle of pills out of the kitchen drawer.*) Give him a couple of these.

He pours some pills into Lance's hand, then recaps the bottle. Lance fills a glass with water and goes over to his uncle. Thaddeus is too distraught to realize where the pills have just come from.

LANCE: Here you go. Now you just rest. (*Thaddeus takes the pills. Lance takes the glass from him and goes back to the kitchen area. To Sebastian—*) I've never seen him this upset. You've got to help me calm him down, Sebastian.

SEBASTIAN: How?

LANCE: We'll reason with him. Tell him everything that's happened this morning has been one big fluke. Maybe he'll calm down some now that he's taken those tranquilizers and we can—

SEBASTIAN: Uh, Lance . . .

LANCE: What?

SEBASTIAN: Those weren't exactly tranquilizers.

LANCE: What were they?

SEBASTIAN: Don't get excited. I don't think they're supposed to have much effect on humans at all.

Thaddeus hears this and perks up.

LANCE: What do you mean they're not supposed to have much effect on humans? What kind of pills were they?

SEBASTIAN: Just some pills I used to give my dog for worms.

LANCE: The dog that died?

Sebastian nods. Thaddeus rises abruptly.

THADDEUS: What is all this?!!!

SEBASTIAN: Don't worry. Those pills will just speed up your heartbeat a little and put some strain on your kidneys.

THADDEUS: Strain on my kidneys?!!!

SEBASTIAN: Settle down, Uncle Thaddeus.

THADDEUS: You tell me to settle down when you've just given me dogworm pills that are going to speed up my heartbeat and strain my kidneys?!!!

He grabs up his cell phone.

LANCE: What are you doing?

THADDEUS: I'm calling for an ambulance. *(Sebastian heads toward the bedrooms.)* Where are you going?

SEBASTIAN: You're obviously distraught. I'm going to see if I can find you some more medicine.

Sebastian exits. Thaddeus sputters, unable to speak.

LANCE: He's only kidding, Uncle Thaddeus. Why don't you just sit down and rest? I'm sure everything's going to be all right.

THADDEUS: You're insane. Both of you are insane. (*He suddenly grabs his chest.*) Oh, no!

LANCE: What?

THADDEUS: I can feel my heartbeat speeding up.

LANCE: Would you like me to get you anything? (*Thaddeus looks at him abruptly.*) No, I mean like a glass of water or something.

THADDEUS: No.

LANCE: How about some brandy?

THADDEUS: Well . . .

LANCE: Brandy it is. (*He goes to get it.*) I'm sure you'll be all right if you just take it easy until the pills wear off. Just don't do anything to excite yourself. I'm really sorry about this. (*He approaches Thaddeus and hands him the glass.*) Here you go.

THADDEUS (*drinks, relaxes a little*): Yes, that's better. Much better.

He starts punching numbers on his cell phone and takes another sip as Sebastian enters.

SEBASTIAN: Here's some more medicine, Uncle Thaddeus. I think it might— (*He stops dead, then shouts—*) Uncle Thaddeus!! (*Thaddeus jumps and almost spills his drink.*) What's that you're drinking?!!

THADDEUS (*meekly*): Brandy.

SEBASTIAN: Brandy!!! Uncle Thaddeus, you've ruined your kidneys!! You should know better than to drink alcohol after taking those pills!

THADDEUS: How should I know what's the proper drink, I've never taken dog pills before!

SEBASTIAN (*rushing to the kitchen area*): Quick, Uncle Thaddeus, come over here and drink some water. (*Thaddeus rushes over. Sebastian fills a large glass and hands it to him. He drinks.*) Hurry, hurry. (*Thaddeus finishes. He's panting as he hands the glass back to Sebastian. Sebastian refills it and gives it back. Thaddeus drinks.*) Quick, quick. (*Thaddeus finishes. Sebastian refills the glass.*) Keep drinking. You've got to keep drinking.

Thaddeus finishes the third glass and hands it back to Sebastian. He's panting more violently now. Sebastian starts to refill the glass.

THADDEUS: No . . . (*gasp*) . . . No more . . . (*pant*) . . . I don't care what happens, I can't drink anymore.

SEBASTIAN: Okay, start walking around the room. (*He grabs Thaddeus' arm.*) Come on, start walking. (*With Sebastian leading him, Thaddeus walks unsteadily around the room.*) I can't believe you would be so irresponsible as to drink alcohol with those pills. You seem to have no sense of self preservation.

THADDEUS (*breathing heavily*): I'm a rich man, Sebastian . . . I swear if I live through this . . . I'll hire hitmen to come in the night and kill you. (*They walk a little more, then Thaddeus stops suddenly.*) Oh, no.

He rushes off toward the hallway.

SEBASTIAN: Where are you going?

THADDEUS: *You* ruined my kidneys, *you* figure it out.

He exits.

LANCE: You've done some terrible things before, but this is the worst. My uncle comes to stay with us, I ask you not to pull anything, and you damage him for life.

SEBASTIAN: He'll all right.

LANCE: All right? You've ruined his kidneys. You saw the way he had to run to the bathroom.

SEBASTIAN: That's just because of all the water he drank.

LANCE: Well, I'm going to throw away those pills right now. Where are they?

SEBASTIAN: On the counter.

LANCE (*going over*): I don't see why we kept these around here in the first place. (*He grabs the pill bottle.*) Hey, these are just vitamin C tablets.

SEBASTIAN: How 'bout that?

LANCE: But you made my uncle think . . . Listen, you'd better tell him the truth. (*Thaddeus enters, carrying a suitcase. We can tell it was hastily packed by the fact that clothes are hanging out at the edges.*) Wait, Uncle Thaddeus. Don't go.

THADDEUS: I'm not staying in this den of horrors another second.

LANCE: No, wait. (*He grabs him.*) I can't let you go like this. Sebastian has something important to tell you. (*Thaddeus stops. Lance looks at Sebastian.*) Are you going to tell him, or will I?

SEBASTIAN (*relenting*): Okay, I will. Look, Mr. Montgomery, you realize I wouldn't really give you anything that would hurt you, don't you?

THADDEUS (*it's the last straw*): I don't know, any pills you'd give a dog for worms can't be all that good for me!! (*He tries to exit as Lance holds him.*) No. Get away from me.

He pushes free and exits.

LANCE: Now look what you've done. My uncle will never forgive me.

SEBASTIAN: I didn't—

The door bursts open. Thaddeus stumbles through as he is pushed. Enter the three members of the Radical Homeless Youth

Brigade, weapons at the ready.

MITYA: Trying to escape, you capitalist swine?

Lance starts for his uncle. Edgar points his gun at him.

EDGAR: Nobody move.

TOMÁS: Thaddeus P. Montgomery, you are hereby arrested in the name of the Radical Homeless Youth Brigade for crimes committed against the workers of the world.

THADDEUS (*moans*): Oh, no.

Curtain

ACT THREE

Same scene as before, a little later. The hallway door is now closed and the couch has been pulled across it, blocking it. Also, several boards have been nailed across the door. As the scene opens, Edgar is standing on the couch, hammering in the last of the nails. His machine gun is beside him on the couch. Thaddeus is in the chair at Down Left. Mitya stands beside him, pointing her pistol at his head. Tomás is standing approximately where the couch used to be. He, too, is pointing a pistol at Thaddeus. Sebastian is sitting on one of the desk chairs, leaning back against the desk. Lance is on one of the stools at the kitchen counter. Edgar hammers the final nail and climbs down off the couch.

EDGAR: Finished.

TOMÁS: Good. Now we won't have any S.W.A.T. teams coming up behind us. All we have to guard is the front door.

EDGAR: Why don't we board it up, too?

TOMÁS: We need to be able to come and go, get extra food, things like that. There's no telling how long we'll be up here.

THADDEUS (*angrily*): If you think I'm going to just sit around and—

MITYA (*pressing the barrel of her gun against his temple*):

Shut up.

Edgar picks up his machine gun and aims it at Thaddeus.

EDGAR: Let me spray him.

TOMÁS: Not yet.

LANCE (*tentatively*): Excuse me. (*Tomás looks at him.*) Can I ask you a question?

TOMÁS: What?

LANCE: What are you planning to do with us?

TOMÁS: With you, nothing. But as for your uncle . . . (*He walks up to Thaddeus, sits on the arm of the chair, and presses his gun to Thaddeus' head. Thaddeus now has a barrel at each temple.*) Him, we're going to put on trial.

EDGAR: I still think we should execute him right now.

TOMÁS: No, we have to give him due process of law. (*to Thaddeus*) Of course, we could forego the trial if you were willing to make proper restitution for your crimes.

THADDEUS: And just what would you consider proper restitution?

TOMÁS: We've prepared a list. Mitya.

Mitya pulls a sheet of paper out of her pocket, unfolds it, and begins to read.

MITYA: Articles of Restitution in the Case of Thaddeus Montgomery. *Article One*: Mr. Montgomery shall go on nationwide TV and make a speech, not less than thirty minutes in length, denouncing his former capitalistic acts. *Article Two*: Mr. Montgomery shall turn over all his factories to the men and women who operate them, for the better good of the proletariat. *Article Three*: To show his remorse for a wasted life of capitalistic pursuit, Mr. Montgomery shall commit suicide by hanging himself to a high branch. *Article Four* . . .

THADDEUS: Um . . . about that *Article Three* . . .

TOMÁS (*sternly*): Quiet. There will be no interruptions during the reading of the Articles of Restitution. (*to Mitya*) Continue.

MITYA: *Article Four*: Mr. Montgomery shall sell everything he owns and give the money to the poor.

TOMÁS (*to Thaddeus*): Do you agree to these conditions?

THADDEUS: Certainly not!

TOMÁS: Then we have to have the trial. (*He backs away from Thaddeus.*) Mitya, bring me one of those stools. We have to turn this place into a courtroom. (*Mitya gets one of the stools from the kitchen area as Tomás surveys the room.*) I need something I can use as a podium. Edgar, move that filing cabinet over here. (*to Lance*) You help him. (*Edgar shoves the books off a small filing cabinet, and he and Lance start to drag it toward Right Center.*) That's right. I want it right over here.

While this is going on, Thaddeus rises and starts to tiptoe toward the door.

SEBASTIAN (*innocently*): Where are you going, Uncle Thaddeus?

Thaddeus is startled and stops. Several guns are quickly aimed in his direction.

TOMÁS: Get back in your seat. (*Thaddeus returns to his chair.*) I ought to blast you.

THADDEUS (*petulantly*): I was just stretching my legs.

EDGAR (*moving toward Thaddeus*): Why don't you let *me* stretch his legs?

TOMÁS: No, there'll be plenty of time for that sort of thing later. First we have to grind him under the wheels of justice. (*The stool and filing cabinet are now set up like a judge's bench. Tomás goes and sits on the stool and rests his hands on the filing cabinet to test its height.*) Just right. (*Tomás glances at the area to the right of his podium, then looks around the room.*) Bring that chair over here. (*He indicates one of the desk chairs. Edgar brings it over to him.*) Put it down there. (*Edgar places it beside the filing cabinet.*) That's where the witnesses will sit. (*He looks around.*) Now all I need is a gavel. (*An idea occurs to him. He takes off his shoe and bangs it on the filing cabinet, a la Khrushchev.*) Perfect.

SEBASTIAN: I take it you're going to be the judge?

TOMÁS: That's right.

SEBASTIAN: Do you need a volunteer for prosecutor?

TOMÁS: No, I promised that job to Edgar. He wants a chance to cross-examine Mr. Montgomery.

EDGAR: With a stick.

THADDEUS (*alarmed*): Hey, what kind of a trial are you planning on running here?

TOMÁS: Don't worry. It'll be a fair trial. We want everything legal.

Thaddeus jumps up and scrambles for his phone.

THADDEUS: Then I'm entitled to one phone call!

TOMÁS: Stop him!

Edgar and Tomás jump Thaddeus and start to wrestle with him.

THADDEUS (*into phone*): Hello! Hello!

Lance starts to come to Thaddeus' aid, but Mitya points her gun at him.

TOMÁS: Give me that.

He wrenches the phone from Thaddeus' fingers. Edgar drags Thaddeus across the room.

THADDEUS: No! I'm entitled! Everyone gets a free phone call!

Edgar throws Thaddeus into his chair. He is now towering over him, his machine gun pressed to his head. Tomás, still standing at Downstage Right, pulls his pistol and aims across at Thaddeus.

TOMÁS: You try another stunt like that and I'll *let* Edgar stretch your legs. (*At this moment, the door opens and Frederick enters. He's smiling as he strides confidently into the room, slamming the door behind him; but his smile disappears as he stops abruptly, noticing the scene. He looks quickly from gun to gun, then, being no fool, he turns and heads for the door, trying his best to convey the impression that he has simply entered the wrong apartment.*) Freeze! (*Frederick freezes.*) Who are you?

Frederick turns to face him and pretends he does not speak English.

FREDERICK (*rapidly, with a thick accent*): *Pardon, Monsieur, vous ne me voulez pas, je ne parle pas Anglais.*

He shrugs his shoulders and starts to leave.

TOMÁS: I said, freeze! (*Frederick freezes again. Tomás goes up to him.*) If you don't understand English, how come you know what "freeze" means?

FREDERICK (*feebly*): I'm a quick study?

TOMÁS (*shoving into the room*): All right, who are you?

FREDERICK: I work for Mr. Montgomery. I'm his valet.

TOMÁS (*indignant*): What? (*He turns to Thaddeus.*) You have a valet? A manservant? A sheep in slave's clothing? (*to Frederick*) Your testimony will be very important at the trial.

FREDERICK: What trial?

TOMÁS: We're putting Mr. Montgomery on trial for crimes against the proletariat.

FREDERICK (*brightly*): Really?

TOMÁS: Yes. And we need your testimony.

FREDERICK (*delighted*): Oh, okay.

THADDEUS (*shocked*): Frederick! (*He sputters as he tries to come up with some crushing condemnation, then he blurts—*) You're fired!

FREDERICK: That's fine with me. (to *Tomás*) Where do I sit?

TOMÁS: Anywhere.

Frederick heads for one of the stools at the kitchen counter.

FREDERICK (*in obvious good spirits*): Hello, Sebastian. Lance.

SEBASTIAN: Hello, Joe.

Frederick sits, then turns to Sebastian.

FREDERICK: Have I missed anything?

SEBASTIAN: No, we're just getting ready to start.

TOMÁS (*back at his podium*): As I was saying—

The door bursts open and Mrs. Vail enters the room carrying several pieces of luggage.

VAIL (*happily*): Here I am, Thaddeus. All packed and . . .

Her words trail off as she sees the armed intruders.

TOMÁS (*angrily*): Edgar, close that door and lock it! I'm getting sick of people just wandering in here. You'd think they didn't have anyplace else to go on a Saturday.

VAIL: What is this, a robbery?

TOMÁS: Just shut up, lady, and find someplace to sit. (*grumbles to himself*) If it gets any more crowded in here, we'll have to send out for more chairs. (*to Edgar*) You got any cobalt charges?

EDGAR: One.

TOMÁS: How strong?

EDGAR: Enough to blow up half this building.

TOMÁS: Good. Attach it to the door. From now on, nobody comes or goes without my say so.

Edgar unhooks the small bomb from his belt and begins to attach it to the door.

VAIL: I demand to know what's going on here.

TOMÁS: It's none of your business. Sit down.

VAIL: I'll have you know, I own this building.

There is a brief pause as Tomás' face registers surprise, then, with extreme distaste, he says—

TOMÁS: *A rent collector!*

EDGAR (*turns and shouts automatically*): All rent collectors should have their skin peeled off by giant, starving cockroaches!!

Mrs. Vail, wide-eyed with astonishment, backs away from Edgar.

VAIL: Thaddeus, who are these people?

THADDEUS (*despairing*): I have no idea.

SEBASTIAN: They call themselves the Radical Homeless Youth Brigade. They're sort of a cross between a political action committee and a motorcycle gang.

VAIL: Well, if it's money you want, just name your price. My fiancé is one of the richest men in the country.

THADDEUS: Shut up, woman!

TOMÁS: I don't care how rich he is. We came here to put Mr. Montgomery on trial, and that's what we're going to do if it takes all day. Now, siddown!

Mrs. Vail grabs the remaining desk chair and pulls it over beside Thaddeus' chair.

THADDEUS (*cringing away from her*): Do I have to sit here?

TOMÁS: Yes! And I don't want any more interruptions out of you, either. Mitya, come over here. (*Mitya goes to the side of the filing cabinet opposite the witness chair.*) You're going to serve as the bailiff and court secretary. Take down everything that's said. (*He pulls a piece of paper out of his shirt pocket and gives it to her.*) Here are the charges against Mr. Montgomery.

MITYA: Okay.

Toma bangs his shoe on the filing cabinet.

TOMÁS: This court shall now come to order in the case of the Workers of the World versus Thaddeus Montgomery. Mr. Montgomery, approach the bench. (*Thaddeus hesitates and Edgar grabs him by the collar and drags him over. Tomás turns to Mitya.*) Read the charges.

MITYA: Thaddeus P. Montgomery—you're charged with committing capitalistic crimes against the proletarian heroes who are committed to lives of virtual slavery in your corrupt factories. How do you plead?

THADDEUS: Not guilty.

EDGAR: Objection.

TOMÁS: Sustained.

THADDEUS: What do you mean, sustained? In can plead not guilty if I want to.

TOMÁS: Mr. Montgomery, you're out of order. Return to your chair. (*Edgar points his gun at him as an added enticement to go. Thaddeus returns to his seat.*) The prosecuting attorney will now state the case against the defendant.

EDGAR (*vehemently*): The defendant is a swine of the lowest caliber.

Pause.

TOMÁS: Would the prosecuting attorney care to elaborate on that?

EDGAR: Oh . . . Okay . . . The defendant is a swine of the lowest caliber because he lives off the sweat of the women and children who slave in his factories. He drives fancy cars while we take the bus. He wears fancy clothes while we buy off the rack. But the tide is turning, Mr. Montgomery. We are going to overcome! We'll drive the swines like you from the factories! We'll take over your businesses! We'll take over your bank accounts! We'll have our way with your daughters!!!

He suddenly stops and everyone turns to stare at him. There is a brief pause.

TOMÁS (*clearing his throat*): *Ahem* . . . I think what the prosecuting attorney is trying to say is—

SEBASTIAN: I think we all know what he's trying to say.

TOMÁS: Very well, then. The defense may now answer the charges of the prosecution.

THADDEUS: What charges? They were the ravings of a lunatic.

TOMÁS: Are you wishing to change to an insanity plea?

THADDEUS (*rising*): Not *my* insanity. *His.*

He points to Edgar.

EDGAR: *My* insanity is not questioned here.

THADDEUS: This whole trial is a farce. If you had any evidence, you'd present it.

FREDERICK (*raising his hand, speaking eagerly*) Call *me* to the stand. *I'll* give you evidence.

Thaddeus whirls around.

THADDEUS (*angrily*): Frederick!

FREDERICK: Joe's the name. You fired me, remember?

THADDEUS (*suddenly conciliatory*): I was joking. (*He turns to Tomás with an ingratiating little smile.*) We often share little moments of levity together.

FREDERICK: You want to hear about abuse of workers?

Just ask him how much he used to pay me.

THADDEUS: I was going to give you a raise, you ungrateful little serf!!

TOMÁS (*banging his shoe*): Order! Order! Mr. Montgomery, I'll not allow any disturbances in this court! One more outburst and I'll have you restrained.

Thaddeus grumbles to himself and sits down.

SEBASTIAN: Your Honor, may I interject at this point?

TOMÁS: If what you have to say has some bearing on this case.

SEBASTIAN: It does.

TOMÁS: Proceed.

SEBASTIAN (*rising*): Your Honor, it is obvious that Mr. Montgomery has neither the legal acumen nor the mental capacity to answer the charges against him. Therefore, with the permission of the court, I would like to take over as his defense council.

THADDEUS: No! You can't! I object!

TOMÁS (*bangs shoe*): Overruled. (*to Sebastian*) Your point is well taken. (*solemnly, to the assemblage*) This court hereby appoints Sebastian Dumas to be legal council for the defense.

SEBASTIAN: Thank you, Your Honor.

THADDEUS (*grabs his head and moans to himself*): Nooo . . . Nooo . . .

SEBASTIAN: The first thing I'd like to do is move for the immediate dismissal of the charges against Mr. Montgomery.

Thaddeus stops moaning and looks up, surprised.

TOMÁS: On what grounds?

SEBASTIAN: On the grounds that if you execute Thaddeus Montgomery, you will be doing irreparable damage to the radical cause.

TOMÁS (*sternly*): If you're attempting to make a mockery of this court, let me just warn you—

SEBASTIAN: Not at all, Your Honor. I'm quite serious. Surely, as one of the leaders of the radical movement, you must be aware of the value of martyrs.

TOMÁS: Yes.

SEBASTIAN: Well, if you execute Mr. Montgomery, you'll be guilty of giving capitalism it's first great martyr. The entire capitalistic world will lower its flags to half mast and proclaim him a fallen hero. The New York Stock Exchange will erect a statue in his honor. School children will start wearing "We Love Thaddeus" T-shirts and forming little industrial cartels. Is this what you hope to accomplish with your trial?

TOMÁS (*in horror*): No!

SEBASTIAN: Then I submit that your only choice is to dismiss the charges against Mr. Montgomery.

TOMÁS: But we can't allow him to go unpunished.

SEBASTIAN: I'm not suggesting that. (*He thinks for a second.*) Look, why don't you just cut off a few of his fingers and be done with it?

THADDEUS: What!?!

TOMÁS: I don't think a few fingers are enough.

SEBASTIAN: All right then—a hand. But that's as high as I can go.

THADDEUS: Don't listen to him! He doesn't represent me! I want a new lawyer!

SEBASTIAN: Be quiet, Uncle Thaddeus. I'm trying to plea bargain.

THADDEUS: You told them to cut off my hand! What

kind of plea bargaining is that?

SEBASTIAN (*turning to Tomás*): Your Honor, this trial has obviously been a great strain on Mr. Montgomery. I'd like to ask the court for a brief recess so I can give him some medicine to calm his nerves.

He pulls the pill bottle from his pocket.

THADDEUS (*going berserk*): Aaarghh!!

He jumps Sebastian and starts choking him.

TOMÁS: Stop him! (*He and Edgar rush over and try to pull Thaddeus off of Sebastian, who is now struggling on the floor with Thaddeus' fingers around his neck.*) Get off him! . . . Let go! . . . You're only hurting yourself!

THADDEUS (*gleefully*): No, I'm not. Look at him turning purple.

They finally pull Thaddeus off and throw him back into his chair. Edgar picks up his machine gun which he had tossed aside to help Sebastian, and aims it at Thaddeus. Sebastian rises unsteadily, coughing and gasping for air.

TOMÁS (*to Edgar*): If he moves, shoot him. (*turning to Sebastian*) Are you all right? (*Sebastian nods, then tries to speak.*) What? What are you trying to say?

SEBASTIAN (*with great difficulty*): As . . . (*choke*) . . . As

Mr. Montgomery's legal council . . . (*gasp*) . . . I would like to . . . (*choke, gasp*) . . . throw him on the mercy of the court. (*He lowers himself into his chair.*) The defense rests.

TOMÁS (*to Edgar*): Do you have anything to add?

EDGAR: No.

TOMÁS: This court will now take a brief recess to consider the verdict.

He goes back to his bench. Edgar remains where he is, his gun pointed at Thaddeus. Mitya hands Tomás the transcript of the trial and he sits looking through it.

VAIL (*desperately*): But they can't do this. If they execute you before we're married, then I won't be able to inherit your money. (*She puts her hands on him.*) Thaddeus, do something.

THADDEUS: Don't touch me. Isn't it enough that I'm going to be killed?

FREDERICK (*pulling his chair forward*): Buck up, Thaddeus. Maybe you'll have better luck with the appeal.

THADDEUS: Don't talk to me, you valetarian Judas. My only solace is the fact that they'll have to kill all of you, too, so there won't be any witnesses.

FREDERICK: Oh, I don't think they'd do a thing like

that.

TOMÁS: Mr. Montgomery, approach the bench. (*Edgar grabs Thaddeus and drags him up to Tomás.*) This court finds you guilty of crimes committed against the workers of the world. Due to the undesirability of turning you into a martyr, however, I'm having a little difficulty setting your sentence.

SEBASTIAN (*raising his hand*): Um . . . Your Honor?

TOMÁS: Yes?

SEBASTIAN: I have a suggestion.

He goes and whispers into Tomás' ear. Tomás looks at Thaddeus, then leans over and looks across the room at Mrs. Vail.

TOMÁS: That's perfect! Edgar, disconnect the bomb. I'm sending you out to get a preacher.

EDGAR: What for?

TOMÁS: Sebastian has suggested the perfect punishment. We're going to force Mr. Montgomery to marry the rent collector.

Thaddeus is too stunned for words.

MITYA (*appalled*): That's inhuman!

TOMÁS: I know. That's what makes it so perfect.

EDGAR (*grumbling*): I don't think it's enough. We should at least pluck out his eyes or something.

TOMÁS: No, this is better. Which would you consider worse: to have your eyes plucked out, or to be married to *her*?

He points to Mrs. Vail. Edgar looks at her, then turns to Tomás.

EDGAR: I'll get the preacher.

TOMÁS: Good. We'll have him perform the ceremony right here. I know they don't have a license, but there should be enough witnesses here to make it legal.

VAIL (*throwing her arms around Thaddeus*): Oh, Thaddeus!

THADDEUS (*breaking free*): That does it! That does it! That's all I can stand!! I've suffered things in this madhouse today that no man can bear! I've been brutalized and robbed, I've been fed dogworm pills and listened while a bunch of wild-eyed, ignoramus radicals have threatened me with everything from mutilation to death! But I will not—repeat: *WILL NOT*—sit here and listen to you threaten me with marriage to the daughter of Quasimodo!!

TOMÁS (*timidly*): Calm down.

THADDEUS: I'll not calm down!

He advances on Edgar.

EDGAR (*meekly, backing away*): I've got a gun.

THADDEUS: Gun, bah! (*He jerks the machine gun away from Edgar.*) All right, you, dismantle that bomb. And be quick about it. (*He whirls the gun toward Tomás and Mitya.*) Drop your weapons!

They do.

VAIL (*rushing to him*): Darling!

THADDEUS (*aiming the gun at her*): Back off!

VAIL: But I just want to kiss you.

THADDEUS: I can't think of a more perfect case for justifiable homicide.

TOMÁS: Um, Mr. Montgomery, I hope you haven't taken anything seriously that's happened here today.

THADDEUS: Shut up. (*to Edgar*) Hurry up, you.

EDGAR: I have to be careful. This is a cobalt charge bomb with a fiberglass core. It'll blow up if I try to disconnect it too quickly.

THADDEUS: You're lying. You can't use a cobalt charge with a fiberglass core.

EDGAR: You can if you reverse the ionization.

THADDEUS (*suddenly interested*): Who taught you to do that?

EDGAR: I figured it out myself.

THADDEUS: And it works?

EDGAR: A six ounce charge could incinerate this building.

THADDEUS (*walking over to him and leaning down to examine the bomb*): It's ingenious. The fiberglass core would make it stable, and the cobalt charge would make it cheap to produce. Have you ever considered marketing it commercially?

EDGAR: There's money in this sort of thing?

THADDEUS: Certainly. I own four munitions factories, and they can barely keep up with the demand. (*warmly*) We're a warlike race, Edgar. There'll always be a market for cheap methods of destruction.

EDGAR: I never thought about making money before.

THADDEUS: If you came to work for me, I'd start you

out at forty thousand a year.

EDGAR: With stock options?

TOMÁS (*aghast*): Edgar!

THADDEUS: With stock options.

EDGAR: Deal.

He shakes hands with Thaddeus.

THADDEUS: Is that thing disconnected?

EDGAR: Yes. Once you pull the fiberglass from the core, it's perfectly harmless.

THADDEUS: Ingenious. I predict a bright future for you, my boy.

He pulls something out of his pocket and begins to write.

EDGAR: What are you doing?

THADDEUS: Writing you a check. (*He tears it off and hands it to him.*) You can consider this an advance on your salary.

EDGAR (*looking at the check*): Wow! This is a lot of money. Do you think I should sink all of this into a good growth stock, or should I diversify? What's the commodities market like right now?

TOMÁS (*totally disillusioned*): Edgar! You're talking like a capitalist.

EDGAR (*waving the check*): I've finally got some capital!

THADDEUS (*to Edgar*): Let's have lunch. We have a great deal to discuss.

They head for the door.

VAIL: But Thaddeus, darling . . .

Thaddeus and Edgar exit with Mrs. Vail in pursuit.

TOMÁS (*testily*): Come on, Mitya. Let's get out of here.

MITYA (*to Lance*): I'll see you around . . . often.

Mitya and Tomás exit.

FREDERICK: Do you guys mind if I stay over a couple of days?

SEBASTIAN: No, we'll be glad to have you.

FREDERICK: Thanks. (*He looks at his watch.*) I'll be back later this afternoon. Right now I have to meet Lisa for lunch.

SEBASTIAN: Okay, have a good time.

FREDERICK: Bye.

He exits. Lance and Sebastian are left alone. Sebastian looks at Lance and smiles.

SEBASTIAN: Well, that was fun. What should we do now?

Lance just stares at him a moment, then says—

LANCE: Sebastian, I can't live like this anymore.

SEBASTIAN: Everything turned out all right.

LANCE: That's what you always say.

SEBASTIAN: It's always true.

LANCE: But I'm exhausted!

SEBASTIAN: Go take a nap. You'll feel a lot better.

LANCE (*firmly*): No. I'm not going to be put off this time. For once, I'm taking a stand. You've had things your own way around here for too long. From now on, I'm not paying your share of the rent and your share of the food, and I'm not going to put up with your bringing specimens in here all the time. And you're going to have to get a job. I'm through being a patron. From now on,

I'm going to start living like a normal person.

SEBASTIAN: Okay.

LANCE (*surprised*): What?

SEBASTIAN: I said, okay.

LANCE (*suspiciously*): What do you mean by that?

SEBASTIAN: I mean I always knew it would come to this someday. A person can't be a patron all his life. And you've grown up a lot in the last couple of days. Frankly, Lance, I'm proud of you.

LANCE: Is this one of your tricks?

SEBASTIAN: Not at all. Look, maybe I did take advantage of you and stretch it out as long as I could, but I knew that sooner or later you'd get tired of supporting me.

LANCE: And it doesn't make you mad that I want you to get a job?

SEBASTIAN: I could never be mad at you, Lance.

LANCE: That's great, Sebastian. Listen, where's the newspaper?

They both glance around.

SEBASTIAN: I don't know.

LANCE: Never mind. I'll run out and get a new one, then we can look through the want ads together.

SEBASTIAN: Okay.

LANCE (*going to the door*): I'll be back in a minute.

He exits. Sebastian retrieves a phone book from his desk and sets in on the coffee table. He looks up a number, then pulls out his cell phone and dials.

SEBASTIAN: Hello, New York Times? I'd like to take out a classified ad. Wanted immediately: roommate to share comfortable, two bedroom apartment. Reasonable rates. Apply in person, Sebastian Dumas, Northstar Apartments . . . That's right.

Sebastian hangs up the phone and gets his volume of Saki, settles into his chair, and begins to read. Lights fade as—

Curtain

BLINDNESS

A Play in One Act

A blind man sits alone on a park bench. He wears dark glasses and has a white cane. A woman approaches. She is in her mid-thirties and fairly plain. She carries a sack lunch.

WOMAN: Is anyone sitting here?

The blind man feels around on the seat beside him.

BLIND MAN: No.

The woman sits. Pause.

WOMAN: Nice weather we're having.

The man holds his hand out to his side, palm up, feeling for rain.

BLIND MAN: Apparently.

WOMAN: Do you come here often?

The man turns his head to the left and to the right; he leans forward and turns left and right again, then sits back in his original position.

BLIND MAN: It's hard to tell.

(*Pause*)

WOMAN: You're not very talkative, are you?

BLIND MAN: Not very. (*She starts to speak, but he cuts her off.*) And don't ask if I've read any good books lately.

WOMAN: You don't have to be so touchy.

BLIND MAN: Look, lady, why don't you sit someplace else? It would be difficult for me to find another bench.

WOMAN (*cheerfully*): I could tell you didn't want to be alone. That's why I came over. (*Smiles pleasantly and opens her sack.*) I'm on my lunch break. I work at Haammerlick and Bruester—you know, the attorneys? I'm just a secretary, but I hope to learn the business someday. Anyway, I usually eat my lunch alone in the office because I can't afford to go out like the others. I just sit and stare out the window and watch the world go by while I eat my sandwich. (*Pulls a carefully wrapped sandwich from her sack.*) Would you like some? (*She holds it out. He leans toward it, sniffs a few times, then shakes his head no.*) I made it myself.

BLIND MAN: So I guessed.

WOMAN (*cheerily begins eating*): Anyway, like I was saying, I decided that today was such a beautiful day, there's no sense eating at the office, so I just packed up my lunch and headed for the park.

BLIND MAN: It's not safe in this park, lady. Lots of dope fiends and crack addicts. They'd kill you for a bite of your sandwich.

WOMAN: I'm safe here with you.

BLIND MAN: Don't count on it.

WOMAN (*smiles and looks around*): I like to come sit in the park. It takes your mind off things. You can just sit and daydream and nobody bothers you.

BLIND MAN: That hasn't been my experience.

The woman chews her sandwich for a moment, then, abruptly—

WOMAN: Do you think I'm overweight?

The question startles him. He lifts his fingers tentatively in her direction, then lowers his hand back into his lap.

BLIND MAN: I hesitate to find out.

WOMAN: I joined this exercise group one time. On the first day, they told us to wear loose fitting clothes to class. If I'd had any loose fitting clothes, I wouldn't have had to be there! And exercise videos are worthless. I've sat and watched those things for hours. I even bought a treadmill once. I got the kind that was electric, so I could leave it running, day and night, even while I was at work—

BLIND MAN: Isn't it time for you to be back at work now?

WOMAN: Oh, no. They never care when I come back. (*Looks wistfully at the falling leaves.*) I was supposed to attend college, but I had to go to work to help out my family. I've thought about buying a pet. With a dog or a cat, you never have to be alone. You've got something that loves you and can't get away. Do you have any pets?

BLIND MAN: I have a bird. I don't consider him a pet so much as a potential meal.

WOMAN: You should get married.

BLIND MAN: How do you know I'm not?

WOMAN: No ring. (*Takes a bite of her sandwich.*) Are you Jewish?

BLIND MAN: Only on my parents' side.

WOMAN: I have to marry a Catholic.

BLIND MAN: That's a relief.

WOMAN: I don't think my family would approve if I married a man who was sort of Jewish. (*Looks at him sideways.*) I don't suppose you'd consider converting?

BLIND MAN: To Catholicism?

WOMAN: Would your family disapprove?

BLIND MAN (*fiddles with the button on his shirt sleeve*): I don't think I have much family.

WOMAN: I know I do. (*Wrinkles her nose.*) Cousins, uncles, brothers, aunts. Around Christmas we have a full house. (*Turns to him.*) You don't celebrate Christmas much, do you?

BLIND MAN: Not every year.

WOMAN: I love Christmas. The lights, the presents. It's a shame you don't get Christmas. What do Jews get?

BLIND MAN: Shafted.

WOMAN (*takes another bite of her sandwich*) I think it's best not to be bitter in life, don't you?

BLIND MAN: I haven't given it much thought.

WOMAN: Boy, I sure have. That's all I ever think about, how it's best not to be bitter in life. You can't just go around feeling bitter about all the things you ought to, or you wouldn't have time for anything else.

They are both silent for a moment.

BLIND MAN (*quietly*): What are you bitter about?

WOMAN: Oh, lots of things. Like you being Jewish and I have to marry a Catholic. Like everybody else gets to go out for lunch, and I have to sit in the office and eat these lousy sandwiches. (*Eyes tear up and she begins to lose control.*) Like I was supposed to go to college, and instead I had to stay home and help out my parents, who are Catholic anyway, and how am I supposed to find a husband if everyone I meet is either married or Jewish? (*Stops abruptly; reaches into her bag an pulls out a tissue, then silently packs her trash into her sack.*) It was very nice meeting you. (*softly*) I'll leave you alone now.

She wads up the sack and prepares to go.

BLIND MAN (*quietly, tentatively*): Will you be back tomorrow?

WOMAN (*a catch in her throat*): I could be.

BLIND MAN: I'll be here.

WOMAN: Maybe we could talk again.

BLIND MAN: That would be nice. (*Rubs his Adam's apple.*) You know … I don't see why I couldn't marry a Catholic.

The woman sits very still. She can't quite allow herself to believe what she has heard.

WOMAN: Are you asking me to marry you?

BLIND MAN: It was only a matter of time before you asked me. This is a preemptive proposal.

She looks at him a long time.

WOMAN: You wouldn't mind being married by a priest?

BLIND MAN (*points to his dark glasses*): How would I know?

The woman smiles, a relaxed, tender smile, and takes his hand. She leans back contentedly.

WOMAN: All right, but Christmas we'll have to spend with my folks.

The two of them sit quietly, hand in hand, as the lights slowly dim.

Curtain

LIFEBOAT

A Play in One Act

Scene is a large lifeboat in the middle of a calm sea. In the background can be seen a luxury liner in flames, sinking beneath the surface of the water. In the lifeboat are two men. Each is eating a can of ravioli. Edmund Graves, the man at stage left, has an oar across his lap. Victor Stavenger, at stage right, has one at his feet. Neither man is speaking.

Suddenly, a hand grips the rail. A man pulls himself up from the water; he is sopping wet and breathing heavily.

Stavanger quickly grabs the oar at his feet and leaps to the side of the boat. He begins to beat the man back into the water. It takes many whacks, as the man is struggling for his life. Stavenger beats him about the head, the shoulders, the chest, the hands. Edmund calmly continues to eat his ravioli while watching this outburst. The man over the side never makes a noise; he just struggles silently until he finally disappears into the inky depths. Stavenger sits down and resumes his meal.

EDMUND (*dryly*): I'm glad I got to the boat before you did.

They eat for a moment in silence. The man's head appears once again. Stavenger takes up the oar again and clubs him about the head and shoulders, forcing him back into the water. Once again, it is a long, drawn-out process. When it is over, Stavenger sits.

EDMUND: You know you're using up more calories keeping him out of the boat than you're saving by depriving him of rations.

STAVENGER: It's the principle.

There is a brief pause as they continue to eat; then—

EDMUND: Is this your first voyage?

STAVENGER: No. I sail all the time.

EDMUND: Pleasure?

STAVENGER: Business.

EDMUND: How interesting. What do you do?

The man appears again. His left arm clings desperately to the side of the boat while his right hand waves a fist full of money.

Stavenger takes up the cudgel once again and beats him back into the water. As before, the man never says a word, just struggles in desperate silence until he finally disappears. Stavenger sits.

STAVENGER: Sorry.

EDMUND: That's quite all right. You were about to tell me what you do for a living.

STAVENGER: Oh. I write travelogues. You know, 'The Joys of an Ocean Voyage.' That sort of thing. (pause) How about you? Done much traveling yourself?

EDMUND: I've been on a few cruises. (*He peers into the water where the man has disappeared.*) None like this, though.

STAVENGER: I know. This has been pretty rough. This reminds me of that story—you know—six people in a boat, who do you eat first?

EDMUND (*lifting his oar menacingly*): Don't expect any votes until you let some more people in the boat.

Stavenger sets aside the can of ravioli he had been eating and looks up at the sky.

STAVENGER: It'll be night soon.

EDMUND: I guess so.

STAVENGER: At least the weather is calm. I wonder if they'll be able to find us. The rescue ship I mean.

EDMUND: I don't know. Do you think the captain had time to get off a distress call?

STAVENGER: I hope so. We ought to be okay as long as we stay in the shipping lanes. Someone will come along eventually.

A hand stretches up from the water, fingers outspread like a leafless tree; trembling, it grabs the rail.

Stavenger runs to the edge of the boat and violently stomps the fingers. It takes a while, but the hand eventually disappears. Stavenger stands with his foot poised a moment, then resumes his seat.

EDMUND: I didn't want to disturb you, but isn't that a rescue ship over there?

STAVENGER (*squinting at the horizon*): Maybe. It'll do anyway.

He lifts his can of ravioli, finishes the last few bites, and tosses it aside. Edmund picks up one of the bags.

EDMUND: Anything you want to take with us?"

STAVENGER: Nyah. (*peers at the horizon*) How soon do you think they'll be here?

EDMUND: About fifteen minutes. Maybe less.

Stavenger nods as if the answer satisfies him. He leans back against one of the bags and clasps his hands behind his head.

STAVENGER: You know, it wasn't such a bad cruise after all. I definitely think I'll recommend it to my readers. (*props his feet up onto a bag*) I'm going to grab a quick nap. Wake me when they get here.

EDMUND: Okay.

Edmund begins putting things into the bag he is holding. Stavenger closes his eyes and smiles peacefully. He remains in this pose as—

Curtain

ART MUSEUM

A Play in One Act

Scene is the interior of an art gallery. Abstract paintings and modern sculpture line the walls. The main focus of the exhibit is a shoulder-high piece of abstract sculpture, roughly T shaped. A man stands examining it closely.

A woman approaches and stands next to him, admiring the sculpture. She is young and attractive, with soft blond hair hanging past her shoulders. The man leans toward her. He seems very self-assured, almost cocky.

MAN: Hello. (*She looks at him, then turns back to the sculpture. He smiles and begins with a know-it-all attitude which quickly fades.*) Ah, yes … (*motions to the sculpture*) … I think this piece is very . . . er . . . symbolic.

WOMAN: Of what?

MAN (*struggling*): Why . . . er . . . um . . . of Life.

The woman looks at him, then walks away without speaking. A second man standing nearby has noticed the exchange.

SECOND MAN: Pssst . . . Pssst . . . PSSST!

MAN (*startled*): I beg your pardon?

SECOND MAN (*casually*): I said 'pssst'.

MAN: Oh.

The man looks at the second man as if he is crazy. He moves subtly away. The second man follows him.

SECOND MAN: Pssst.

MAN (*angry now*): What do you want?

SECOND MAN: You're going about it all wrong.

MAN: I don't know what you're talking about.

SECOND MAN: Sure you do. Listen, I'm just trying to help you. (*looks toward the woman*) Watch this. It's all in the terminology. (*He straightens his collar and saunters up to her.*) Hello. (*She nods but does not speak.*) You like this piece?

WOMAN: Mm-hmmm.

SECOND MAN: Personally, I consider it a masterpiece of existential epistemology delineating the futility of human endeavor.

WOMAN (*impressed*): Wow. You really know a lot about art."

SECOND MAN: I should. I happen to be a professional critic.

WOMAN: Really? (*shyly*) I'm studying art at the university.

SECOND MAN: How interesting. Why don't we go to your place and discuss it further? Perhaps I'll buy you dinner.

WOMAN: Okay.

He puts his arm around her shoulder and starts to lead her away. He turns back to the first man and loops his thumb and index finger into an "OK" sign as they leave. The first man is now very excited. He can hardly wait to try out what he has learned. He sees a tall redhead admiring the sculpture. He approaches her.

MAN: You like this piece?

SECOND WOMAN: Very much.

MAN: Personally, I consider it a masterpiece of existential epistemology delineating the futility of human endeavor.

SECOND WOMAN: Say what?

MAN: Um . . . I, uh . . . er . . . I think it's very symbolic. Why don't we go to your place and I can explain further? Perhaps I'll buy you dinner.

SECOND WOMAN: You're paying?

MAN: I'm paying.

She suddenly grabs him and throws him forward.

SECOND WOMAN: All right, buddy. Up against the wall. (*flips out a badge*) Detective Miller, Vice. You're under arrest for solicitation.

She handcuffs him and leads him out. They nearly bump into two people just then entering the gallery, an artist and his agent. The artist is noticeably upset; the agent tries to console him.

AGENT: Calm down. Everything is fine. So the critic is a little late. Don't worry, he'll be here.

ARTIST: Why should I have to peddle my work like soap, anyway? I'm surrounded by plebians. Just this morning, I caught a man putting out his cigarette on one of my sculptures. Claimed he thought it was an ashtray. Uncultured swine! And I hate to think about what that dog did to my yard exhibit. (*He clasps his head.*)

AGENT: It's all going to be worth it when the critic sees this. (*motions to the T-shaped sculpture*) You really have surpassed yourself this time.

ARTIST (*calms down as he admires his work*): It truly is a masterpiece, isn't it?

AGENT: Certainly. Now let's go see if we can find that

critic. He may be in another part of the gallery.

While they were talking, a man has stepped up to the sculpture. He watches them leave, then turns his attention back to the piece of art. He leans close to the sculpture, squinting his eyes. He rubs the base to check its texture. He leans back and strokes his chin, viewing the work critically. He leans forward, grabs the end of one of the T bars, and moves it slightly up and down.

Suddenly, it breaks off into his hand. He looks quickly from side to side to see if anyone has noticed. He tries desperately to put it back on. He presses it. He twists it. He spits on the contact surface to see if this would make it stick. Nothing seems to work. Now he hears the voice of the agent coming back into the room.

AGENT: It's right through here . . .

The man looks around desperately and pitches the broken piece of sculpture behind a nearby work of art. The artist and the agent enter with the critic. They are visibly shaken when they see the sculpture. Neither can speak. The guilty man stands with his eyes tightly closed and his shoulders hunched as if he is expecting an explosion.

CRITIC (*after a moment*): Magnificent! (*The man's eyes pop open. The agent looks at the critic in shock. The artist continues to stare at the sculpture.*) Gentlemen, I have a confession to make. I actually came up here last night to look at your sculpture, and quite frankly, I was unimpressed. But now that you have removed that eyesore from the left side!

Well! I think I can say, without fear of contradiction, that the concept is revolutionary.

While the critic has been talking, the artist has remained in shock, but the guilty man now begins to smile and even looks a little proud. The agent is calculating and recovers quickly.

AGENT: We knew you would like it. You should have heard him this morning. He knew there was something wrong, but he just couldn't quite decide what. Then, at about noon today, it hit him: remove the eyesore from the left side. It seemed so simple once he had the answer. (*turns to the artist*) Isn't that true, Pablo?

ARTIST (*coming out of a daze*): Um, yes . . . of course. That's the way it happened. Yes.

CRITIC: Well, it was a stroke of genius. Pure brilliance.

The guilty man now stands casually with his hands in his pockets. He ducks his head in an "aw, shucks" pose.

CRITIC: Come along, young man. We have business to discuss.

The artist and the critic walk out, followed by the agent.

The guilty man is now very proud of himself. He looks around, head held high. He steps up to the piece of art, views it favorably for a moment, then reaches up, breaks off the other arm, and tosses it away. He views the sculpture critically, nods approvingly, then walks off, whistling a happy tune.

Curtain

BANNERS AND FLAGS

A Play in One Act

Scene is a barren wasteland after the apocalypse. No plant life dots the horizon, no noise disturbs the silence. At center stage, a slight mound reveals itself to be the metallic door to an underground bomb shelter. A man walks alone through the cold, dead world. His face betrays weeks of hunger and fatigue. He squints at the rise of ground ahead of him, stumbles over to it, and drops to his knees. He tries the bolt; it does not budge. He presses harder, then stops.

LARRY: Hello in there! Can anybody hear me? (*He picks up a rock and beats it against the surface of the metal.*) I say! Can anybody hear me?

ALFRED: They can hear you, all right. (*Larry turns, startled. The man who stands before him resembles a leper: his skin is horribly ravaged, his clothes are in tatters, his scalp covered with open sores. Yet in spite of his diseased appearance, he is surprisingly strong and agile. He carries a cloth bag over his shoulder and is holding a long staff which serves as his walking stick.*) They can hear you, but they won't answer. They never answer.

LARRY: Who are you?"

ALFRED: Alfred. Alfred Cavanaugh. Who are you?

LARRY: Larry Douglas.

ALFRED: Pleased to meet you, Larry. (*He holds out a twisted hand in greeting. Larry hesitates.*) Ahhh, still squeamish, I see. That's all right. You'll get over that soon enough. (*He sits cross-legged on the ground and digs through his pack.*) So tell me, Larry, where are you from?

LARRY: Washington.

ALFRED: No, I mean lately. Since the bomb.

LARRY: Oh. (*pause*) I've been in a shelter some miles from here. We were close to running out of food, and things began to get nasty. Someone was killed. I left to find a new shelter.

ALFRED: That's too bad. (*His bag rattles as he continues to search its depths.*) The shelters never open up until they run out of food. That's the only time I ever get any company.

LARRY: What are you doing above ground?

ALFRED (*pointing*): That's my shelter there. My neighbors and I chipped in to build it a long time ago. When the warning came, I didn't get here in time. They had already sealed themselves in. I beat on the door, but they wouldn't open it.

LARRY: That's monstrous.

ALFRED: It's human. (*He finds what he was looking for in*

his bag.) Here it is. (*He pulls out a chunk of bread and tears it in half.*) Care to join me?

LARRY (*dubious*): If you haven't been in a shelter, where did you get that?

ALFRED: I found it among the rubble of a grocery store.

LARRY: Doesn't it have radiation poisoning?

ALFRED: Probably.

LARRY (*disgusted*): No, thank you.

ALFRED (*smiling*): I forgot you're still squeamish. (*He contentedly begins to eat.*) Now, where was I? Oh, yes. After I found the shelter was locked, I went to hide in a cave I know of, not far from here. It protected me from most of the fallout. That's where I live now. But I come visit the shelter every day. (*He pops the last morsel into his mouth.*) Now tell me about yourself. I haven't had anyone to talk to in weeks. It really gets lonely up here, waiting for an occasional person to emerge.

LARRY: What do you want to know?

ALFRED: Why not tell me about the people in your shelter? Were they your neighbors?

LARRY: No. It was a government shelter. I was doing work for the military.

Alfred, impressed, makes a gesture which encompasses the world around them.

ALFRED: Then all of this is your doing.

LARRY: Now, just a minute . . .

ALFRED: Oh, don't get angry. The military did what they had to do. But you said things got nasty in your shelter?

LARRY: Yes. Rations were short and everyone was on edge. Someone was accused of stealing food, and they killed him.

ALFRED (*frowning*): They shouldn't have done that. They went about it all wrong. There are rules for that sort of thing. You've got to follow the rules. If you don't, you've got chaos and anarchy, and that translated into Sin.

LARRY: What are you talking about?

ALFRED: Sin. I've been doing a lot of thinking about it, and I've got it all figured out. Look here, suppose a man sees another man on the street and kills him. That's a sin, right?

LARRY: I'd say so.

ALFRED: And it's a crime, right?

LARRY: Yes.

ALFRED: But suppose he sees that same man on the other side in a war. Then he's expected to kill him. Now what's the difference between the two cases? In both, he kills a man he doesn't know, yet in once case he's sinning, and in the other he's not. Why?

LARRY: In the case of the war, he has to kill him. He's the enemy.

ALFRED: But I can't just step up to one of my enemies on the street and kill him. So it's not that he's the enemy. Come on. What is it?

LARRY: I don't see what you're driving at. Is it the fact that he's on foreign soil?

ALFRED: That's nonsense. Suppose there was a man I didn't like. Could I just follow him onto foreign soil and kill him?

LARRY: Of course not.

ALFRED: Then think. What's the difference?

LARRY (*considers*): I know what it is. When a man kills someone in war, it's not his decision to commit the act. He's following the orders of his superiors.

ALFRED (*exasperated*): Now you're just being ridiculous.

The Mafia assassin is just following orders. Do you think he's committing a moral act?

LARRY (*tired of this game*): Why don't you just tell me? What *is* the difference between killing a man in the street and killing him in a war?

ALFRED (*smugly*): Banners.

LARRY: Banners?

ALFRED: And flags. That's what the man in the war has that the man in the street hasn't. Banners and flags. And songs, of course. You can't have a truly satisfactory war without a good, rousing anthem.

LARRY: What are you talking about?

ALFRED: The moral justification of war. It's really very simple. I didn't have much else to do while I sat around up here, so I spent most of my time thinking, and eventually it all became clear to me: flags are magic. They really are. Just think about it a minute. Would any sane young man leave his family and his girlfriend to go kill strangers in a foreign country if he weren't under the influence of magic? Of course not. But where does this magic come from? It must be from the banners and flags. You see, they represent civilization. That's why I was concerned to hear that the people in your shelter were committing acts of murder with personal motives. That's a threat to civilization itself. You must never kill out of anger or need. That's a sin. We all know it's a sin. Murder is a very naked crime. You have to clothe it in banners and flags, salutes and slogans. If we lose our patriotism, civilization will die. We will sink back to the savagery of the animals, who kill for hunger rather than for banners.

LARRY (*standing*): You're insane.

ALFRED: Why? Because I know the value of civilization?

LARRY: I'm not going to argue with you. I've wasted enough time here as it is.

He starts to turn away.

ALFRED: Wait. Where are you going?

LARRY: To find some food. I haven't eaten in nearly three days.

ALFRED: You don't have to leave. I can get you all the food you want right here.

LARRY (*scowls*): No thanks. I'm not interested in radiation poisoning.

ALFRED: No. I mean good, clean food.

LARRY: How?

ALFRED (*motions to the shelter*): We know they've got

food down there. All we have to do is convince them to come out and share it with us.

LARRY: And how do we do that?

ALFRED: By plugging their air vents.

LARRY: That will make them come out, all right. But how do we convince them to share their food?

Alfred reaches into his bag. He pulls out a small wooden club and a large hunting knife. He looks very menacing as he brandishes the club in his right hand and the knife in his left. Larry looks at him, then down at the shelter, then back at him.

LARRY (*cont.*): Let's do it.

Alfred nods. Larry drops to his knees and starts filling the air vents with sand. Alfred shoves the knife into his belt, slips the club under his arm, and reaches back into his bag. He comes out with a white piece of cloth, smeared with blood. He ties two corners of it to the end of his staff and plants the staff into the ground so that it resembles a makeshift flag. Larry looks up and sees Alfred standing at attention, saluting the banner.

LARRY (*cont.*): What are you doing?

In one swift motion, Alfred takes the club from under his arm, whirls around, and strikes Larry between the eyes. Larry collapses into the dirt. Alfred then takes the knife and begins to sharpen it against a stone.

ALFRED: Yes, it gets really lonely up here, waiting for an occasional person to emerge. But I'll never go hungry. Food is always provided for those who know the magic of the flag.

He is very solemn as he stares at Larry and continues to sharpen the knife. The only noise in the cold, dead world is the sound of the blade scraping back and forth, back and forth, against the rough edge of the stone.

THE END

ABOUT THE AUTHOR

Mark Pearce is an author/playwright whose plays have been produced on the New York stage and around the country. Formerly Resident Playwright of the New Ensemble Actors Theater of New York, his play Asylum was listed in The Burns/Mantle Theater Yearbook: The Best Plays series.

In addition to his work in the theater, he has had stories published in various literary journals in the United States, England, and Canada. His first published story was nominated for a Pushcart Prize and was selected as Granfalloon magazine's "Story of the Year." He was subsequently nominated for a second Pushcart.

The year 2023 saw the publication of his debut novel, *Tobias and the Isle of Justice.*

Printed by Amazon Italia Logistica S.r.l.
Torrazza Piemonte (TO), Italy